TALKING OF
DICK WHITTINGTON

Albert Grant, Esq., M.P.

Talking of
Dick Whittington

by

HESKETH PEARSON

and

HUGH KINGSMILL

Drawings by Marjory Whittington

" The pleasure which there is in life itself."
(*Wordsworth*)

LONDON
EYRE & SPOTTISWOODE

First published 1947

Printed in Great Britain for
Eyre & Spottiswoode (Publishers) Ltd.
15 Bedford Street, London, W.C.2.

CONTENTS

CONTENTS

A BOOK ON LONDON

One day early in 1944 it occurred to Marjory Whittington that there was room for a book on London, and she approached Douglas Jerrold, who asked Hesketh Pearson if he would supply the text to Mrs. Whittington's drawings. A contract was duly signed by the interested parties; Pearson completed his Life of Wilde and failed to begin his book on London. Some time previously, when he was discussing a third travel book with Kingsmill, they had decided that eld and increasing indolence put anything like the enormous area covered in the Scottish Pilgrimage of *Skye High* out of the question; and they were reluctant to cope even with the more restricted area of *This Blessed Plot*. "We should be able to manage London," said Kingsmill. "Something topographical, reaching back into the past, I suppose."

"And forward into the present, perhaps."

"I was at Highgate the other day, and thought of Dick Whittington with his cat—a young chap in a jerkin, you know, a stick over his shoulder, and hanging from it a handkerchief with his few belongings. What about 'Talking of Dick Whittington' for our title?"

"An admirable title. It commits us to nothing, neither of us knowing anything about him."

As Pearson was still down at Battle in Sussex, they shelved the project for the time being; but in the spring of 1945, Pearson's failure to begin his book being more pronounced than ever, he suggested to Kingsmill that his book on London might become theirs, a suggestion which Kingsmill passed on to Graham Greene. "Graham is working with Douglas Jerrold, and will tell him all about it before we turn up," said Kingsmill.

On Friday afternoon, April 27, Pearson and Kingsmill called at Eyre and Spottiswoode, where they found Jerrold and Greene together.

KINGSMILL: Graham will have told you why we called.

JERROLD: He has told me nothing. Why have you called?

KINGSMILL: Hesketh feels that the book he is supposed to be doing for you would, if it were written, be just a glorified guide-book.

PEARSON: There are dozens of them about, crammed with details about famous literary and historical persons who have lived in this or that house and that or this street.

KINGSMILL: "It is not generally realised that Hogarth resided . . ." "It is easy to imagine Tom Moore lightly tripping . . ."–That is the kind of thing the prospect of which is keeping Hesketh awake and the realisation of which would send his readers to sleep.

JERROLD: Do what you like, Hesketh. I leave it entirely to you.

KINGSMILL: That opens the way to the next point. Namely, that Hesketh and I want to write about London along the same lines as our books on Scotland and England. So why shouldn't Hesketh's book be ours?

JERROLD: You will stick to London?

PEARSON: And Rochester.

JERROLD: It's quite a good idea. Go ahead.

KINGSMILL: By London we shall, when desirable, understand Southern England. Southern England has meant
London during these flying-bombs and rockets, so it is
only fair that London should mean Southern England for a
change. And Yarmouth.

JERROLD: You mean where Steerforth was drowned?

KINGSMILL: Precisely.

JERROLD: Anything about Dickens will naturally come
well from you and be well received by me.

GRAHAM GREENE (*mistrustfully*): How do you two do
your books?—I can't understand. Does one take the pen at
one sentence, one at another?

PEARSON: We make notes as we go round, from time to
time putting down anything that has struck us as interesting or amusing, and recording the details of chance
encounters as soon after as possible. So far as our own
conversations are concerned, they are sufficiently faithful
reports of our own conversations. Then, when enough
material has been accumulated, we put it together, Kingsmill holding the pen, I striding up and down, or seated, as
the case may be.

KINGSMILL: In short, Graham, everything is factual,
except that we suppress our good deeds in the interests of
good taste, and so as not to make ordinary mankind
despair—

PEARSON: Or vomit.

KINGSMILL: Or vomit. Such then, Graham, is our pro-
cedure, and of its fruits it is not for me to dictate your
opinion.

11

The war against Germany having come to an end on a date agreed between various unspecified Government departments, and Pearson's landlord returning to his Battle home, Pearson came up to London, and he and Kingsmill met for dinner at the Wellington in Fleet Street on Monday, July 30.

Hardly had they settled themselves, when Pearson unburdened himself as follows.

"It is probably because I have been living in the country for more than six years that egotism in all its variety and in its starkest manifestations has been forced on my attention. The country is favourable to the growth of egotism. In towns people are compelled to keep their egos in check by constantly brushing against several thousand other egos, each of which is too busy to encourage the development of the rest. But in the country egotism festers in solitude and erupts in society; and, contrary to the general assumption, countrymen are not only excessively self-interested but, once got going, the world's long-distance talkers. After listening to them for a year or two, and studying the different forms their self-absorption took, I decided to write an Anatomy of Egotism. But I abandoned it on the ground that such an analysis would itself smack of egotism, and decided instead to start a Society for the Suppression of Anybody who Speaks without Stopping for More than Two Minutes, as I am doing at present.

"Of course, we are all egotists more or less; but the reasonable egotist does not expect other people to be as interested in him as he is in himself; the unreasonable one does, and is consequently a menace to social life and spiritual tranquillity. My book would have dealt chiefly with the last kind, personified by such superficially dissimilar historical personages as Napoleon, Dickens, Cromwell, Tennyson, Hitler, Hugo, against whom one could place, as reasonable egotists, Johnson, Wellington, Fielding, Lincoln, Shakespeare, Pearson and Kingsmill.''

KINGSMILL: I . . .

PEARSON: I have classified as follows the four main types of egotists, as they appear in social intercourse. The first type is the man or woman who continually breaks into any conversation, merely because he or she cannot bear to be ignored. The second takes no interest whatever in anything that does not directly concern himself, and maintains a peculiarly aggressive silence when alien subjects are being discussed. The third has something to say on everything, and says it incessantly; his views are as trite to his listeners as they are striking to himself, and the sound of his own voice delights him as much as it jars on the rest of the world. The fourth is the man who is full of self-pity and whose misery colours his view of the universe. When he has finished the tale of his own ailments and misusage, he complains of the weather, the government, the food, and the latest fashion, and foretells disaster in every field of human endeavour. Such is egotism as I have learnt to know it in the country. How and why I have escaped being infected by it, I leave to others to explain. Well, that's enough to go on with.

KINGSMILL: It's enough to stop short with.

Pearson, the whole of whose life since his marriage in 1912 had been spent in St. John's Wood, when he was not elsewhere, had now settled down in Priory Road, to which address Kingsmill, with a full sense of the importance of the occasion, proceeded on the morning of Friday, August 3. As he mounted the steps, he caught a glimpse of Pearson as man of letters, bending gravely over his writing-desk in the bow window.

"You will excuse the disorder," said Pearson, as he welcomed his friend. "Labour is difficult, and indeed, so far as I am concerned, impossible. But I picked this up just now out of that pile of junk. It should interest you as a glimpse of Dickens off duty. It's from the Hardman papers, and is a letter to Sir William Hardman from Shirley Brooks."

Kingsmill took it and read:

"Dickens sent me a good story, but it is for the wise only. The moral is that in describing anything you should keep yourself well in hand, and not travel out of the record. A Methodist preacher was expatiating on the goodness of the Almighty in sending His only begotten Son to save us, and he went on, 'Think, my brethren, of this great, this unspeakable goodness—His Loved Son, His only Son, His Dear Son, to whom He looked as the prop of His declining years.' "

Later in the day, after an early tea, Kingsmill suggested that they should inaugurate their survey of London by getting out of it in the direction of Cockfosters, from which they could walk to High Barnet; and they set forth.

PEARSON: Goldhurst Terrace is just up there, and Abbey Road is just down here.

KINGSMILL: Practically twenty-four years since you took me up to 88, Abbey Road for the first time, and already five years since that month I spent in your flat in Goldhurst Terrace. Everything so peaceful except for the bombs, and everyone so friendly. Five years!

PEARSON: Very testing.

SUMMER HARMONY

They took the tube to Cockfosters, Pearson somewhat sceptical about the wonderful walk promised him by Kingsmill, who had been there the previous summer. A few minutes from Cockfosters station they entered a wood of scattered trees with a little lake below them, and though Pearson couldn't go all the way with Kingsmill, who was already speaking of "this forest," he freely admitted that it reminded him of the western part of Hampstead Heath. Through the trees to their left they saw a distant gasometer, which dispirited them for a moment, but on consideration they agreed that the modern fashion of not being able to enjoy the works of God unless the works of man were in complete harmony with them came from people who had to find an excuse for not being able to enjoy either.

KINGSMILL: Besides, one likes to be reminded of man wherever one is. A gasometer is a bad expression of a good idea.

PEARSON: And it would be a damned good expression of a

15

thundering good idea if one was pushing one's way through parrots and pampas in the upper reaches of the Amazon.

Hardly had they passed the lake when they met a youth and girl who wished to be directed to it. "That is perfectly simple," said Pearson, expanding himself with the effect of creating a background from which Kingsmill could watch and wonder. "You . . ." and he told them at some length to continue in the direction in which they were going, Kingsmill suddenly at one point supplementing his information without deflecting from Pearson any of the esteem and gratitude visible on the countenances of the youth and girl.

"We shall pass this way but once," said Pearson, as they went on. "Any good thing that we can do, let us not neglect, for we shall not pass this way again."

In front of them lay a grassy common cut by a road which disappeared over a hill, and to their right there was a thick wood which in the intense brightness of the afternoon threw black shadows on the ground. It was a hot and cloudless day, and they diverged into the coolness of the trees, but not wishing to be swallowed up in the dim recesses which stretched before them, swerved back to the road, which they reached safely some ten minutes after abandoning it.

At the top of the rise there was an old mansion, and two old ladies sitting in the front garden under a large tree. "Do you think they appreciate it?" said Pearson. "It's mid-eighteenth century. Johnson struggling up here would have passed it. That house next to it is earlier–Queen Anne. Panelled rooms probably–a graciousness never found nowadays. The wing is mid-Victorian. Even that is older than

us. ('Of course it is,' Kingsmill muttered irritably.)
Look at that dear old church! Let's go in."

They stood in the churchyard, Kingsmill noting it was
the parish church of Monken Hadley, was called St. Mary
the Virgin, and dated from 1494, but had been rebuilt in
1898. Beyond a wall they saw the upper stories of a
beautiful late seventeenth-century house. It had a red-tiled
roof, and the tiles were sunk and uneven. "The perfect
harbour for a storm-tossed life," said Pearson. "Give me
this house and a certainty of ten more years on earth with
an adequate unearned income, and I would surrender my
present position and my future prospects." "So would I,"
said Kingsmill, "but who's giving us all this in return for
our future prospects, to say nothing of our present
position?"

"Anyhow, that's the offer," said Pearson.

They turned from the church, and were immediately
attracted by a large house standing back from the road with
a drive bordered by a flower-garden. There was a glimpse
of country to the right of the house, and as the windows
were shuttered, they passed through the gate and went
forward to see what the view was like. A lady emerging
from the front door, they took her into their confidence,
and she, after a slight pause, very charmingly offered to
show them the house and grounds. They were delighted
with the house, privately reflecting that it too would serve
for the remaining span of their lives; and the view from the
tiled terrace at the back was even lovelier than they had
expected, the garden descending towards a valley beyond
which on the opposite slope a corn-field shone in the sun,
above it a fringe of trees black against the burning sky.
Not a house to be seen anywhere, and when they exclaimed

how far from London they felt, their hostess, Mrs. De'ath, told them that the foxes came at night and ate the chickens. Shaking hands with them, she said they might explore where they liked, and they walked along a grass-grown avenue between trees and reposed for a while on a massive stone seat, such as Addison, while meditating *Cato*, might have found congenial to his Muse.

ATOMS

Kingsmill, who was working on *Punch*, arranged to meet Pearson for tea on the following Wednesday at the Kardomah in Fleet Street. He had with him a book on Horace which he was reviewing, and said he had realised for the first time that Horace had not spent the whole of his life turning verses and slave-girls over on his Sabine farm. "I knew he was more or less at Philippi," he said, "but round about 1908 that meant nothing to me. Now the Antony–Octavius Axis, and Brutus and Cassius as the United Nations, and Horace unable to think out any convincing reason why his studies at Athens University should be regarded as work of national importance, are all depressingly real."

PEARSON: How wonderfully Brutus's end in Shakespeare transforms into poetry the feeling of a politician when he and his plans come unstuck—

> Night hangs upon mine eyes, my bones would rest,
> That have but laboured to attain this hour.

KINGSMILL (*gravely*): Others also have felt like that.

18

PEARSON (*leaning forward with a disagreeable gleam*): And always with a feeling of self-pity.

KINGSMILL: Oh, very well.

Pearson walked back to *Punch* with Kingsmill, and sat there while Kingsmill finished his review. The Atom Bomb had fallen on the previous Sunday, and as they emerged into Bouverie Street, Kingsmill said he now understood why Stalin had looked so depressed and Truman so merry in the photographs taken at Potsdam. ''Stalin,'' said Kingsmill, ''has always liked science, and now he finds Truman shares his taste, and yet he isn't happy.''

''Are you?'' said Pearson.

''Well, I suppose, as usual in these matters, things will turn out worse than one hopes and better than one imagines.''

Hearing rapid steps behind him, Kingsmill looked round and saw Vernon Bartlett, who appeared preoccupied, and indeed oblivious of his surroundings. So fast was he travelling that he might have outstripped them past recall, had Kingsmill not ejaculated ''Do you know Hesketh Pearson?'' Bartlett slowed down, shook hands, and was gathering momentum again when Kingsmill asked ''What about the Atom Bomb?''

BARTLETT: I'm hoping someone will move an amendment to the King's Speech.

KINGSMILL: What about the wider implications?

''Brrrrrr,'' shuddered Vernon Bartlett, and jet-planed up the street.

Having decided to visit the East End, Pearson and Kingsmill met at the Authors Club in Whitehall Court on
Saturday, August 11, Pearson in a state of great irritation
against Tolstoy, whose *War and Peace* he had been struggling
with for the third time. "I read an expurgated edition in
my twenties," he said. "It bored me. I attempted to read
the Everyman edition in my forties. I couldn't get beyond
the first dozen chapters. Then came all the twaddle about it
in this war, and I determined to give it a final try. I got
through the first volume of Maude's translation and then I
stuck. It is inexcusably dull. A writer who can't engage
my interest in the course of the first five hundred pages
is obviously not the man for me, yet I faced without
blenching and read without quailing Mommsen's *History of
Rome*, Morley's *Life of Gladstone* and Milton's *Paradise Lost*.
Nor is Tolstoy only a crashing bore, he is also a staggering
fool. His views on Shakespeare and Beethoven are those of
an idiot. No such rot has ever been uttered by a supposedly
great man. What he said about *King Lear* and the *Kreutzer
Sonata* should have qualified him for a strait waistcoat.

KINGSMILL: Ah well! it takes all sorts to make a world.

PEARSON: Say what you like about Shaw, he's at least a
better novelist than Tolstoy. I've been reading his novels,
and find them quite amusing.

KINGSMILL: I'd assumed that as even Shaw didn't praise
them, no one else could.

PEARSON: They remind him of his poverty, sense of
failure, and frustration.

KINGSMILL: I understand why they should remind him of

his sense of failure, but I don't see any necessary connection between poverty and bad work. On that basis Wordsworth's "Tintern Abbey" is better worth forgetting than the "Ode on Queen Victoria" which he wrote with his nephew, Bishop Christopher.

THE SEWER

Leaving the Club at about three, they went by underground to Bow Road, along which they walked, admiring its width and the old William the Fourth houses interspersed among more modern buildings. They passed a disused station, the property of the North London Railway, a relic from the mid-Victorian world, which carried them back to the time when railway power dominated the imagination and a Carker was dashed to pieces by a fiery iron steed instead of being disintegrated by an atom bomb. In front of the station was a memorial drinking-fountain, erected by Bryant and May. "That's a striking motto on it," exclaimed Pearson. "*Despice finem*. Despise the end! That's heroic for a commercial concern. Oh—it's *respice finem*. Not so good. Who's that woman on it? What is her precise purpose?" Kingsmill having said she was doubtless the Roman Goddess Vesta, whose name the English had borrowed for matches, and Pearson showing no sign of being impressed by Kingsmill's scholarship, they proceeded on their way, passing the Constitutional Club, a Regency building. A brass plate informed them that it was the headquarters of the Conservative Association, and through the window they saw a number of gloomy aristocrats playing whist.

They delayed outside Bow Church, which had been badly hit, until Pearson had satisfied himself that the east and west older ends were joined by a relatively modern chancel. Two other churches within a short distance looked as if they had been burnt out. "No fire-watchers," said Pearson, "a symbol of the sluggish state into which my church has fallen. I don't blame them for no longer believing in the flames of Hell, but incendiary bombs are a fact, not a matter of faith."

Seven buses, almost but not quite empty, passed them, and they looked at each other with a mild surmise which deepened as a car went by, containing three women and one man, all in evening dress, who seemed amused by the two travellers. "This is a strange region with laws of its own," said Kingsmill. They were emerging into an area which had either never been built on or had recently been destroyed, and nothing interposed between them and the high white clouds that stretched right across the horizon.

PEARSON: It reminds me of a mining village in America—odd houses here and there between brick-kilns and salvage yards.

KINGSMILL: On the whole, a spacious effect—canals and gasometers, wide streets and distant horizons.

Passing a lively small boy with a catapult, who was fortunately concentrating on a poster of a Jap soldier, they stopped a man and asked the nearest way to the Docks. After giving them some instructions too intricate for them even to appear to grasp, the man said "But your best way is by the sewer."

"The sewer!"

"The sewer."

He took them up on to an embankment which ran at right angles to the road, and they saw a wide, grass-bordered avenue which stretched for miles in either direction. Walking along it towards the Thames, admiring the wide expanse below them and the factory chimneys far off by the river, they paused from time to time to look at the houses which skirted the foot of the embankment. Each had its little garden, and the travellers agreed that each garden had something distinctive about it, but, knowing nothing about gardening, were unable to be more specific; except when Pearson, pointing to a trellised arch for roses, separating the garden from the back door, said that it created a little Eden for the owner—a tender and beautiful thought with which Kingsmill found himself unable to compete.

A little way ahead on their right they saw a large building in a green park. Workhouse? asylum? hospital? None of these guesses was correct. It was a pumping-station. This information they received from a workman on the sewer, a solid, cheerful Londoner, and the sound of water being pumped confirmed it. He gave them the points of the compass, which Pearson said he already knew, but listened with interest as the man went on to point out London Bridge far to the west, Blackheath on the southern horizon, Silvertown and Plaistow within measurable distance, and the Docks stretching illimitably eastward. He had, he told them, been working on the sewer all through the blitz. Was it ever hit? asked Pearson, wincing a little, and wishing he had never read Dean Swift. A bomb had fallen on the slope of the embankment, the man said, and caused a bit of damage, but nothing to matter. Pearson heaved a sigh of relief, and they passed on. Below them to the right, against the wall of the pumping-station, stood a little group of men who seemed not to relish being looked at. One of them slipped a book in which he was writing into his coat pocket, and the others stared suspiciously at the travellers. "Betting chaps," Pearson murmured to Kingsmill. "They think we're 'tecs, and as we're not armed, we'd better get a move on." They quickened their steps. "It's a fine boulevard, this," said Pearson, "and not a soul in sight. This is at least a quiet walk, even if it isn't a country one." "It would be a quiet walk if we continued it," said Kingsmill, "but as West Ham station's over there, according to that chap, let's go by train." Leaving the sewer, they went by a short cut to the station, where they learnt that if they got out at Plaistow, they could take a bus to Silvertown. Standing on the platform, uncertain whether they really wished to go to Silvertown, they allowed a train which was packed with troops to leave without them, and looked with nostalgia at an empty train travelling in the opposite direction, and marked "Ealing." But another Ealing train coming in, they felt their morale stiffening, and dismissed its occupants as snobs and sybarites.

A SOOTHING PROSPECT

On the bus for Plaistow they passed through a district which had been badly knocked about. "Poor old Churchill!" cried Kingsmill. "Those were happy days for him. And, after all, he took a chance, just as much as you or me.'' Leaving the bus at the beginning of the Dock district, they found themselves on what Kingsmill called a lengthy bridge and Pearson a short viaduct, from which they surveyed vast factories, towering cranes, great ships in dry dock, and in the midst of all this phantasmagoria, hardly discernible, a mean church, with a hybrid tower-spire, and an air of witnessing to Christ in a muffled undertone.

A bus took them down to the Thames, where they noticed a delightful park fronting the river, and asked its name of some children who were playing on a pier. ''They *call* it Woolwich Park,'' piped a little girl non-committally, and being given a shilling rushed off to a whelk-stall, the rest of the pack after her in full cry.

As Pearson and Kingsmill walked away, Pearson re-marked ''What a lot of rot is talked about the degeneracy of urban populations! Cockney kids are far more alive and attractive than country brats going about with lowering sodden looks and a stone ready to hurl at any bird as bright and happy as those kids.''

''The other day,'' said Kingsmill, ''I read that Doctor Ley, the Nazi labour chief, claimed that as a peasant born of farming people he had sound political instincts. I am glad his rural counterparts over here have never got into power.''

In Woolwich Park, leaning back on a seat, they looked over the river at a hill which appeared to Kingsmill very leafy and beautiful, and which he learnt with surprise from Pearson was Greenwich Park. ''Very sylvan,'' murmured Pearson, puffing at his pipe. ''What with sewers and this soothing prospect, I don't know when I've spent a more restful afternoon.''

25

On the bus, Kingsmill, asked for his fare, said "Town, please." "What?" asked the conductress. "London," said Kingsmill. "Where?" asked the conductress, whereupon Kingsmill pulled himself together and said "Charing Cross." The conductress smiled tolerantly and helped them off the bus at Plaistow.

When they got out at Charing Cross, and were walking along Whitehall Court, Kingsmill remarked on the grim, preoccupied air of the people passing by. "There's no doubt," he said, "that the West End is much gloomier than the East. I remember noticing the same contrast many years ago, after spending some hours in Stepney. Here everyone has a position to keep up, and if possible improve, contacts to make, and connections to consolidate. A wearing life."

THE CAFE ROYAL

Colin Hurry asked Malcolm Muggeridge, Pearson and Kingsmill to lunch with him at the Café Royal on August 18. "I love being a guest of yours, Colin," said Kingsmill, "because I know I shall have all the amenities which Somerset Maugham describes so accurately and which, when I read him, I despair of ever encompassing by my own efforts—no doubt the effect he wants his readers to get. Here, for example, is a bottle of—let me see—Balaton Traminer. To me, at least, that has a Somerset Maugham ring."

"You read Maugham with pleasure," said Pearson severely; "yet I've never heard you say anything amiable about him."

"I sometimes *feel* amiable about him, but the words refuse to come."

Emptying his glass, Kingsmill appealed to Colin to confirm him in his belief that the world was already on the high road to recovery. Colin smiled gently, and Muggeridge, laughing tolerantly, told how he had recently been motoring from Paris to Brittany, taking gasolene and cigarettes with him to pay his hotel bills. "It's coming here, too," he added, "and probably in a year or so. You agree, Colin?" Colin, after amending and amplifying Muggeridge's doleful forecast, agreed; and the agreement between them went on for a considerable time, Pearson eating somnolently and Kingsmill impatiently. "This isn't conversation," Kingsmill interrupted at last. "Politics isn't conversation. Economics isn't conversation. I don't know what they are, but I do know what they aren't. Pardon my heat, Colin, but I've been suffering a lot lately, and feel like Johnson when in similar circumstances he exclaimed : 'Alas!' Alas! How this unmeaning stuff spoils all my comfort in my friends' conversation.'"

"Anyhow, this prattle of yours cures insomnia," said Pearson. "In which respect it has the same effect on me as the blitz had on a great friend of mine, Douglas Jefferies. He hadn't had a night's sleep for almost twenty years. The blitz came, and he slept like a log as long as the bombs were falling round him, but started out of his sleep as the drone of the planes died away."

The talk became general in the sense that everyone took a part in it, and particular in the sense that it ceased to deal in generalities, and all parted well content with each other and still better content with themselves.

MARKING THE POETS

The weather deteriorating as August advanced, Pearson and Kingsmill for the time being remained under cover. On August 21 they lunched at the Club, and afterwards Kingsmill suggested that they should join Malcolm Muggeridge and Arthur Dawe. "There they are," said Kingsmill, "looking like Mycroft and Sherlock Holmes, Arthur motionless, massive, and observing everything, Malcolm mobile, arrowy, and missing nothing."

Rather to Kingsmill's surprise, Pearson, as soon as they had seated themselves, remarked "Poets don't show up well as human beings. It pains me to say it, but I say it, Hughie, on the evidence of the quotations from Tennyson's *Guinevere* in your *Matthew Arnold*, which I've just been re-reading. Tennyson's King Arthur is the most revolting figure in all literature, and as Tennyson makes it clear that in his opinion Arthur is the noblest work of God, I repeat that poets give me a pain in the neck."

KINGSMILL: You can't generalise from one instance, even though I've supplied it.

PEARSON: Show me a single poet to whom you can give full marks as a man.

KINGSMILL: Out of a hundred marks I'd give Johnson ninety, because he deserves them, and Shakespeare seventy, although he doesn't. And I'd give Chaucer seventy on his merits.

PEARSON: I wouldn't.

MUGGERIDGE: Nor would I.

KINGSMILL: Why on earth not? What's wrong with him? A most delightful, companionable person, humorous, sympathetic and unpretending. I can't think of anyone I'd prefer on a desert island, though we'd have to come to a reasonable compromise over which particular monarch between Richard II and George VI was to furnish the King's English in use between us.

PEARSON: He may be all you say, but he feathered his nest pretty skilfully. Diplomatic appointments, hogsheads of wine from reigning sovereigns, Custom House pickings, and what not.

MUGGERIDGE: A brilliantly successful civil servant. All the same, I prefer somebody who looks after himself, like Chaucer, to someone like Ernest Dowson, who pretends he's a poet because he's too feeble to pretend he's anything else. And I also prefer Chaucer to Blake.

KINGSMILL: To Blake? Why on earth to *Blake*?

MUGGERIDGE: You must admit that one doesn't write Prophetic Books unless one has tried every other kind of writing, and failed more dismally at each attempt. (*Winningly*) You can't deny *that*.

KINGSMILL: How do you explain that you once told me you'd show Blake to a visitor from another planet as a specimen of human genius?

MUGGERIDGE: On his arrival, and before he was screened.

KINGSMILL: Screened?

MUGGERIDGE: A term used in the Secret Service, meaning investigating someone's credentials and establishing his bona fides. If the visitor passed the test, I'd be prepared to show him some genuine specimens of human genius.

KINGSMILL: It's all in Blake's favour that his wife was happy. He sang hymns on his deathbed, his wife sitting by as happy as he was.

MUGGERIDGE: Happier, I should think. As a deathbed to sit by in a cheerful frame of mind, Blake's was all right.

Pearson, who had been frowning abstractedly during this interchange, exclaimed "I give Shakespeare full marks for everything, a hundred, a thousand, whatever the figure is."

KINGSMILL: But, Arthur, why don't you as a brilliant civil servant straighten out all this tangle?

DAWE: As a civil servant I should require considerably more data than has so far been supplied before making any definite recommendations.

APOCALYPTIC

The weather continuing unfavourable, Pearson and Kingsmill on the following Saturday, August 25, sat in the Club idly forecasting the future. The next war, they agreed, would probably be America and Western Europe v. Russia and the East—the Cousin Countries against the Tartar Terror. The next war but one would probably be Russia and the Brito-Euro Commonwealth v. the Black Block supported by North and South America—a conflict between the Buddha–Christ ethic and the Totem Terror. The next war but two would probably be a Temperate and Tropical

Block *v.* the Arctic-Antarctic Axis, armed with the Stalactite Bomb. The next war but three would probably be Earth *v.* The Rest, after which The Rest could carry on among themselves, and good luck to them.

Lunch over and the rain having stopped, they went into the Embankment Gardens, where they reclined in deck chairs, listening to the band playing *The Dollar Princess,* and vaguely wondering what that melodious phantom of 1910, with her tender conception of leasing and lending, would have made of President Truman's drab and dissonant view of the same subject.

PEOPLE ONE WOULD LIKE TO HAVE BEEN

Two days later Pearson and Kingsmill had tea at the Kardomah in Fleet Street, where, under Malcolm Muggeridge's direction, two of his sons and Kingsmill's son, Brooke, had assembled for refreshment. One of the boys having, out of pure courtesy, asked Kingsmill to repeat a remark he had just made, Kingsmill said that people who asked to have a remark repeated ought to lay down a half-crown deposit, to be forfeited if the remark was not worth repeating. On this the young ones fell silent, and applying themselves in earnest to the food before them, left Pearson and Kingsmill to entertain each other.

"It occurred to me the other day," said Pearson, "that people often tell us who they admire most among the great figures of the past, but never tackle a far more interesting question, namely, which of these famous figures they would most like to have been. An answer to that question would give one a person's real preferences instead of his imaginary predilections."

KINGSMILL: Not wholly imaginary, it seems to me. One can admire a man without wanting to live his life.

PEARSON: Something in that. All the same, the man you would like to be is the real man for you.

KINGSMILL: Only in the sense that he is the man you'd like to be, not because you admire him more than the rest. But who are the men you most admire?

PEARSON: Shakespeare and Beethoven.

KINGSMILL: Would you like to have been Shakespeare?

PEARSON: Not during his *Timon of Athens* phase.

KINGSMILL: Would you put up with the *Timon of Athens* phase in order to have all the others?

PEARSON: No.

KINGSMILL: Would you like to have been Beethoven?

PEARSON: Barring—

KINGSMILL: Barring nothing.

PEARSON: No.

KINGSMILL: Well, that rules out the two men you admire most.

PEARSON: But this is absurd. No one wants to suffer the agonies of others, even in exchange for their raptures.

KINGSMILL: Happiness, then, is what you're looking for in the person you've not yet found?

PEARSON: Yes, but don't forget that this unknown is also famous. That was the point from which we started.

KINGSMILL: Then the man you would like to be is the man who achieved the highest fame compatible with the greatest happiness?

PEARSON: That narrows the list almost to vanishing point.

KINGSMILL: There must have been one or two happy people who were also famous.

PEARSON: I now perceive the entire drift of this discussion. You want to prove that the only man any sensible person would like to have been is that moonshiny, craggy old customer Wordsworth.

KINGSMILL: Not the only person, but one of the few; though I doubt if he is much to be envied in his later years, and personally I would rather have been Beethoven. But, to show I'm not really bad at heart, let me remind you of Andrew Marvell.

PEARSON: Yes, Marvell. I'd be Marvell without any hesitation.

KINGSMILL: Even though he became an M.P.?

PEARSON: Even though he became an M.P.

Malcolm Muggeridge arriving, Kingsmill put the question to him. Malcolm, having first made it clear that it was a choice of infernos, named Chaucer, Johnson ("when all's said") and Wordsworth; and as an afterthought added "And I'd be quite willing to be Shakespeare."

Kingsmill, aware that Shelley, as the lyrical pioneer of Left Wing thought, was not congenial to Malcolm, said "What about Shelley?" Throwing up his arms, Malcolm cried "I'd rather be Julius Streicher, or even Havelock Ellis."

URBANITY

Arriving at Marylebone at 10.10 a.m. on Saturday, September 1, in order to join Pearson for an outing to Chalfont St. Giles, Kingsmill stationed himself by the book-stall. At ten-thirty, the time when the train left, he rang up Priory Road to discover what had happened to Pearson, and learnt that he had set out at nine-thirty. Emerging from the telephone box, he perceived his friend standing by the book-stall, with a look of what appeared to be compressed rage, which mystified Kingsmill, who expected an apologetic air. Approaching Pearson with a forgiving smile, Kingsmill was astounded to be greeted with "I have been sitting in the train since ten o'clock, as arranged at our last meeting, and it is only by the grace of God that I got out in the nick of time." "I say, I'm awfully sorry. I'd clean forgotten. I . . ." "The day's bitched. However, dismiss it from your mind."

Kingsmill having hit on the idea that there might be another train to Gerrards Cross that day, Pearson relaxed, and a few minutes later they were sitting in an empty third-class compartment, Pearson, anxious to illustrate his essential urbanity, recounting a little incident which had happened to him two days before. He was, he said, travelling from St. John's Wood on a 53 bus to Piccadilly when a woman got in and occupied a front seat across the gangway from him. She had flaming bronze hair with a bright golden sheen. He must have unconsciously been staring at it, for when the bus reached Wigmore Street the woman leant over and said "I suppose you think it's artificial." Extremely taken aback, he stammered "That

34

certainly is my impression." "You're quite wrong."
"Then you'd better have it dyed."

"I didn't mean to be offensive," added Pearson. "It
was just that it was the only comment possible."

"Did she reply 'The day's bitched. However, dismiss it
from your mind'?"

Pearson smiled.

A man peering in through the window, Pearson peered
back, and the man went on.

"A near thing," murmured Kingsmill. "One ought to
have a mask for occasions like this—one of those South Sea
devils. Or a rubber baby which squeaks horribly."

"Or my uncle," said Pearson. "At the age of nine, I
was travelling with him from Birmingham to Worcester.
He was a clergyman and a canon. A man tried to enter our
first-class compartment, and was half-way in when my
uncle said to me, urbanely, 'I'm afraid the passenger who
has just left was suffering from scarlet fever.' The man
hastily withdrew. Need I add that there had been no
passenger and *a fortiori* no scarlet fever? I was very much
shocked."

G. K. C. AT HIS BEST

They got out at Gerrards Cross, which they did not much
like as they stood in a long queue waiting for a bus, but
which reminded Kingsmill of G. K. Chesterton at his best.
"It was one of his articles in the *Illustrated London News*

many years ago. The point he was making was that modern philosophers–his term for any journalist with whom he disagreed–have a way of throwing off some insane statement in a parenthesis, as though it were too obvious to be given a sentence to itself. In illustration he quoted someone who had written 'In two hundred years' time (when the individual consciousness is merged in the communal) . . .', and said it was as though he himself were to write 'In sixteen forty-nine King Charles I was condemned to be executed by a Council presided over by Bradshaw (whose mother was a walrus)'; or 'My home is in Beaconsfield, which is seven miles from High Wycombe and four miles from Gerrards Cross (where I ate ninety negroes).' And he very ingeniously followed up these two examples with a piece of propaganda for Irish Home Rule, then an urgent question; his third example of raving lunacy being 'England is bounded on the East by the North Sea, on the South by the English Channel, and on the West by Ireland (whose inhabitants are incapable of governing themselves)'."

A SYMPOSIUM IN THE DESERT

Leaving the bus at the corner of the road which descends steeply to Chalfont St. Giles, they walked down towards the village, admiring the crescent-shaped green in front of The Merlin's Cave and the old square-towered church on the slope beyond. Over lunch at the Pond Tea-House, Pearson, in order to illustrate the importance of economising the truth in social relations, described an

episode during his army days. He and three other officers
had been together for some time in the Mesopotamian
desert, and were getting bored with each other. In order to
jolly them up, he proposed one night in mess that each
should say exactly what he thought of the others, without
any trimmings. The idea was taken up enthusiastically, and
the junior officer was requested to begin. "I'll call them by
their Christian names," said Pearson, "Harold, Vernon
and Sidney. Harold, the junior, starting off, said that
Vernon was an aggressive swine, and that everyone forced
into contact with him cordially loathed him and would
gladly murder him. Sidney, he continued, was a sancti-
monious ass, and all his men laughed at him and despised
him from the bottom of their hearts. He then dealt with
me, and I'll give you his words as nearly as I can remember
them, which is more nearly than I can remember his words
about the other two. 'You think you're charming,' he
said. 'Well, your charm's enough to make a cat sick.
You think you're popular, but if you are it's merely because
you haven't the guts to be disliked. You're too damned
lazy to get anyone's back up, and too fond of a quiet life to
agitate a slug. I quite like you myself, but it would sometimes relieve me immensely to kick your arse.' "

Pausing and looking thoughtful, Pearson said "Of
course Harold was just having a good time—he didn't
mean what he said."

"I see," said Kingsmill. "In fairness to the others, he
had to dish up something against you."

Allowing this interruption to disperse itself, Pearson
continued: "Vernon then got going. Harold, said he, was
a stuck-up puppy and utterly inefficient. 'It may interest
you to know that the men call you Sloppy Sam, and sloppy

is what you bloody well are.' Then he rounded on Sidney. 'You're proud of having nine children. A rabbit could beat you at that, or anything else that requires any spunk— you lousy, psalm-singing bastard.'

"At this point, seeing that Sidney had gone rather grey, and not unmindful that I was next on the list, I intervened and said I thought we'd had enough of it. Silence descended upon us, and lasted for some days."

CHALFONT ST. GILES

After lunch they wandered round the rustic churchyard. It was a grey, calm day; sheep and cows were reposing on the slopes of the neighbouring fields. They entered the church, which was permeated with the antique odour peculiar to village churches, compounded of old stone, pews, prayer-books and vestments.

KINGSMILL: Do you think Milton worshipped here?

PEARSON: I don't think he worshipped anywhere. Communal worship was not in his line.

KINGSMILL: And yet in his youth he must have loved the interior of churches—those wonderful lines in "Il Penseroso," which Gray echoed in his Elegy, but Milton's are more intense, less Anglican.

> "And storied windows richly dight,
> Casting a dim religious light.
> There let the pealing organ blow,
> To the full voic'd quire below,
> In service high and anthems clear
> As may with sweetness, through mine ear,
> Dissolve me into extasies,
> And bring all Heav'n before mine eyes."

38

They went up the street to Milton's cottage, a low, narrow dwelling, 'o'erlaid with black, staid Wisdom's hue,' where they fell into talk with Mr. Beare, the Custodian. He had been there only a few months, he told them, and said it was a strange irony that he, a spiritual descendant of Archbishop Laud and zealous adherent of Latin Catholicism, should find himself tending the shrine of a Puritan heretic. Under his guidance, the travellers examined various portraits of Milton, none endearing. How long did Milton live there? they asked. "Only about ten months," Mr. Beare replied. "He was an evacuee from London, ran away from the Great Plague." Opening a closet door, he indicated book-shelves filled with Puritan apologetics and histories of the Commonwealth, written by Victorians who substituted Gladstone for Cromwell and Tennyson for Milton. Shrill cries from without denoted a horde of schoolgirls impatient for admission. "You had better leave before I let them in," murmured Mr. Beare, whom they thanked for his courtesy, and abandoned half-guiltily to his Puritan calvary.

Crossing the road, they entered the Milton Halt Guest-House, where they enjoyed an excellent tea. A small girl sitting at the next table presented her jam ration on a little dish to Kingsmill, who thanked her with an air of humouring a child's whim by which he had of course no intention of profiting. She and her parents departing, Kingsmill polished off the jam, a little to the disappointment of the proprietress, who had observed what was passing, and had no doubt at one stage hoped to retrieve the contents of the dish. As Pearson and Kingsmill settled the bill, she said "I can see you are a couple of *bons viveurs*."

Returning through the village, they called at the Pond

Tea-House for a cup of tea over which, moved by a reference to Churchill in the evening paper, Pearson remarked that he seemed to be very much in the backwash at the moment, but of course that wouldn't affect his final position. "Even his reiterated attempts to run down Hitler won't affect his final position. Strange that he never saw that by cracking up Napoleon at the expense of Hitler, he was also cracking up Pitt at his own expense."

KINGSMILL: He was in a difficult position, for he ought either to have admitted that his life-long idolatry of Napoleon was misplaced, or that Hitler was as worthy as Napoleon to be idolised.

PEARSON: And that wouldn't have helped when he took over from Neville. I personally think Churchill is much more remarkable than Pitt.

KINGSMILL: Do you remember what Frank Harris wrote about Churchill after the last war? It was just like him, with his extraordinary aptitude for picking a winner and then plunging up to his neck against him, to forecast what Churchill and Churchill alone in our history has done, and then say that he was utterly incapable of doing it. It's a really fine piece of rhetoric, and shows how impressive Frankie could have been in a responsible position if any country had been so irresponsible as to place him in it. He is speaking of Churchill and the other leaders in the last war, and cries that England had "no one to play indicating figure to her millions, no one to imagine, much less to accomplish, the impossible for her sake, and for love of her tear victory from the empty skies and the unsounded seas." If Lincoln or Burke or Churchill or any other accepted orator had brought that off, it would have been in every anthology as his top note.

40

Walking up the hill to the bus stop, they sheltered from a shower under a wall over which some fine trees spread their branches, and looked at the old houses across the road at the top of the incline.

PEARSON: Those houses were there when Milton's coach came lumbering over that rise, though of course part of that pub is more modern. Sad that he never saw those houses in the village below.

KINGSMILL: It was a wretched return to the county of his youth and his loveliest poems—blind and gouty, and the town where he'd wasted his genius now rotting behind him. It has just occurred to me that he never wrote about Paradise Lost.

PEARSON: I wish it had occurred to me when I was ploughing through it at the age of twenty-four. Your meaning?

KINGSMILL: This village was his lost paradise, and these fields the Eden he'd loved before the poet was smothered by the classical pedant and the Hebraic politician.

The bus for Beaconsfield came up and they were carried along narrow, curving roads which had probably not changed their shape in three hundred years. As they walked down towards the station, Pearson waved to the driver of a train going north, and the driver waved back. "Why does one wave to drivers of trains?" he enquired. "I suppose because they can't pull up for a chat. This Common Brotherhood business needs careful handling." The journey back through the countryside was soothing, and they sighed as London closed in on them again.

On September 4 Pearson turned up for lunch at the Club twenty minutes late. Kingsmill, fresh from realising how odious unpunctuality was to his friend, had been anxious, but accepted Pearson's statement that such a happening was so foreign to his nature that it would be pointless to discuss it. As the weather continued uncertain, they forewent their intention to perambulate the Metropolis in the interests of Mrs. Whittington and Douglas Jerrold, but gave half an hour to St. James's Park on their way to Pearson's other club, the Savage. As they crossed the bridge over the lake, Kingsmill said it was a pity G. K. Chesterton had chosen this spot for his proposal to Frances Bloggs. "I love the old balloon," he said, "but he doesn't combine well with love or nature, and still less with both together. His account of his wooing in his Autobiography has never inflamed me. I remember one sentence—'It happened in St. James's Park.' Hardly Romeo." "It occurred in Capulet's garden," murmured Pearson.

KINGSMILL: He speaks of his fright on the bridge and hints that it was a lover's panic. But I suspect it was simply because he was in the open air. According to Maisie Ward in her very readable biography, G. K. C. suffered from agoraphobia—or she may have said he was blessed with it, for she has her own angle where he is concerned.

PEARSON: All his landscapes are unnatural. You never feel that you are in the open. All through the Father Brown stories one is in a gigantic nightmare pantomime—that ghastly old man, or was it a corpse, turning cartwheels against a bloody, reeling sunset which G. K. C. may have thought convincing but which would have flabbergasted a Drury Lane producer.

KINGSMILL: And one can't remember the point of the corpse, or was it an old man, five minutes after the story's finished. It's the same with his autobiography—all prelude and no performance, an impressive caste and no drama. What happened on the bridge? He leads the reader to it, he brings up Frances Bloggs, and advances himself.

PEARSON:

> "O thou day o' the world,
> Chain mine armed neck; Leap thou, attire and all,
> Through proof of harness to my heart, and there
> Ride on the pants triumphing!"

KINGSMILL: Yes, that would have done very well. Instead of which he gives us a lengthy quotation on bridges from an essay by Hilaire Belloc.

PEARSON: He was a shy old boy. He never really grew up.

KINGSMILL: I suppose it was his bulk which misled people.

PEARSON: He hadn't really got the build of a strong man. It was protective tissue, enveloping a perpetual adolescence.

KINGSMILL: Really sixteen all his life. A painful age. I remember a friend of mine, F. H. Fowler, telling me of an appalling day he once had in his 'teens—the sort of thing we've all experienced more or less, usually, thank God, less. He was invited for a week-end in the country, and on arriving found a game of tennis in progress. Asked if he played, he laughed nervously and said, No, he didn't. After a time, to give him something to do, as he was stand-ing at the side of the court, grinning ingratiatingly at any-one who caught his eye, someone suggested that he should tighten the net, which was sagging a little. Full of undischarged nervous energy, he put such force into the job that the net snapped, and while the others were trying to mend it, he was led away by his host, a keen gardener. "A nice bed of dahlias, those," said his host, and Fowler, staring at the wrong bed, gurgled enthusiastic assent. "Not those! *those!*" snapped his host, and led him back to the tennis-court. After dinner, during which he paralysed the few attempts made to engage him in talk, his hostess asked him if he played bridge. Laughing nervously, he said, No, he didn't play bridge. So she led him to a pianola, at the end of the room in which the others were settling down to bridge, and suggested he should play a piece. Presumably she expected him to amuse himself there for a few minutes and then, if her luck turned, fade out and retire for the night. But once seated at the pianola he was too nervous to get up again, and sat there pounding out sound until the bridge-players could bear it no longer and there was a general movement towards bed.

THACKERAY'S HEROINE

The weather continuing to impede free movement, Pearson and Kingsmill passed the following Saturday in a leisurely way, dividing the time between the Authors and the Savage, with a northerly divagation to Piccadilly, where they called at Fortnum and Mason's for Kingsmill's sweet ration, and found it closed, and at the Albany to visit Mrs. Whittington, and found her out. On their way back to the

Authors they were struck by the dilapidated appearance of Carlton House Terrace, which they agreed needed only a naked child tumbling on the steps, a cat or two brooding on the window-sill, and a Madame Defarge glaring out of a broken window in the crumbling stucco, to complete its resemblance to Darnley's House in Stirling, as they had seen it in the summer of 1937.

PEARSON: What would Thackeray think of all this, if he'd just stepped out of the Athenaeum under the impression that he was still in 1863?

KINGSMILL: He'd probably think his quarrel with Dickens had broken out again in a still fiercer form.

PEARSON: How disgraceful it was of Mrs. Brookfield to try and plant a novel of hers on Dickens during that quarrel! Everyone knew Thackeray was madly in love with her, and she must have been reckoning on Dickens accepting it for his paper in order to spite Thackeray.

KINGSMILL: If she had had any foresight, she would have realised that Dickens would exasperate Thackeray much more by rejecting it—what was good enough for Thackeray being, of course, not good enough for Dickens. It was a wretched business for Thackeray altogether. I don't know any episode which better illustrates the fairly general rule that when a woman persuades a man that her husband doesn't understand her, the husband does and the man doesn't.

PEARSON: I've been re-reading Thackeray's novels lately, and she's in all of them—part of Amelia in *Vanity Fair*, a bit of Laura in *Pendennis*, the whole of Lady Castlewood and Beatrix in *Esmond*, and Ethel in *The Newcomes*.

KINGSMILL: Of course Amelia and Laura haven't got much of her, Amelia being, I think, chiefly his wife, and

Laura being colourless, because any colour might have jarred on Brookfield. It was only after the rupture that he could let his real feelings out, and even then there was a hangover from the time when he was incessantly assuring both the Brookfields that his emotions for Mrs. Brookfield were those of a brother or a son. Hence, Laura as Pendennis's sister, until the curtain falls on the bridal night, and Lady Castlewood as Esmond's mother, until Esmond at last realises that the curtain on the bridal night with her daughter is irremediably stuck and that he must make shift with the mother.

PEARSON: And that's why Ethel Newcome is the best of them all, because by that time he'd completely worked the mother-sister theme out of his system.

KINGSMILL: It's touching in Thackeray how feeble his heroes are. True, he makes Esmond and Dobbin colonels, but one doesn't get the feeling that Louis XIV and Napoleon put a price on their heads. And Arthur Pendennis is even less dynamic than his feeder, George Warrington. One really doesn't know which is supposed to be giving the cues to which.

PEARSON: Dickens leaves us in no doubt about that—Nicholas Nickleby and Smike, Martin Chuzzlewit and Mark Tapley, David Copperfield and Traddles. And it must be admitted that Horatio doesn't steal much of the limelight from Hamlet, or Kent from Lear, or, for that matter, Bardolph from Falstaff.

They met again at the Club on Tuesday, September 11. Pearson arriving twenty-five minutes late, Kingsmill asked him whether, as this kind of thing seemed to be becoming less foreign to his nature, it would be profitable to discuss it. Keeping a man waiting half an hour on or near a station platform, Pearson replied, was totally different from allowing him to talk, read, drink or sleep in the comfort of his Club even longer than he had hoped. This point settled, they arranged to meet punctually at 11.30 a.m. the following Sunday at Baker Street station.

Trelawny Irving, an old friend of Kingsmill, had asked them to spend a day at Wellwick, his home near Wendover, and it was with a feeling of relief that the travellers saw London fall away behind them as the train bore them back to Milton's country, and beyond.

At Wendover station they were met by Trelawny, who drove them out to his house. On the way Kingsmill told Pearson that Marley Farm in his *Return of William Shakespeare* was taken from Trelawny's last home, near Chesham. "And a delightful old place it was," he said. "But Wellwick would have suited Shakespeare still better. It's a perfect Elizabethan house." "Jacobean," corrected Trelawny. The road they were following ran under the Chilterns, and presently they turned up a lane to the right and swung round into a spacious semi-enclosed courtyard at the rear of what, as he dismounted, Kingsmill said could only be called a Jacobean pile.

From the living-room the visitors looked out on to a fine lawn. "Charming little lawn-mowers, those," said

Kingsmill to his friend. "Where?" asked Pearson, looking vaguely round. "Those rabbits. Trelawny moves them in their hutches over the lawn, thus keeping it trim and fattening the mowers for subsequent consumption." Isobel Irving coming in at this moment, Kingsmill said "Rabbit for lunch, I hope?" but Mrs. Irving shook her head. "I remembered one of your friends doesn't like rabbits," she said with a smile, "and it would be just like you to bring him down without warning me. So we are not having rabbit to-day." "But this is Hesketh Pearson, and he likes rabbits," said Kingsmill. "It was William Gerhardi, who when he was taking me somewhere for dinner rang up his hostess first to ask if rabbit figured on the bill of fare, and on finding it did said that, in that case, he couldn't come."

After a delightful lunch, based on beef, they returned to the living-room, where the light streamed in from both sides, and the travellers, relaxing after their exertions, lay back in their easy-chairs, gazing comfortably at the vast fireplace where Sir Edmunde Brudenell, the original owner, had roasted his oxen and mulled his ale. Mrs. Irving presently rising to leave them, Kingsmill hoped this did not mean any exacting duties either inside or outside, and Pearson almost stirred in his anxiety to be of help. Accepting her assurance that they would only complicate things, Kingsmill leant back and Pearson remained where he was.

Trelawny having mentioned that he and his wife were shortly going down to Cornwall, Kingsmill asked him if he was related to the Trelawny whose death was so strongly deprecated by twenty thousand Cornishmen. Yes, he said, Sir Jonathan Trelawny was in his mother's family. He told them of the old Cornish mansion where the Trelawnys had lived for many centuries, and then, under pressure from Kingsmill, completed his genealogy with a short account of the Scottish Irvings and a distant glimpse of Ulysses, one of whose descendants, an Ithacan girl, had married his great-grandfather, Shelley's Trelawney.

LEONARD MERRICK

The talk turned to books, and Trelawny having asked if either of them was interested in Leonard Merrick, a writer for whom he had a great admiration, but who appeared to be no longer read, Kingsmill said he was indeed interested in Merrick. "He ought to have figured in my book on Frank Harris," said Kingsmill. "But I didn't distinguish myself over him, and so I suppose unconsciously left him out. When I was eighteen or so I used to read him a great deal, and was especially fond of *The Quaint Companions*, which three or four years later I persuaded Harris to read. The mulatto hero, son of a negro father and an English mother, writes verse and leads a solitary existence, feeling cut off from white men and more especially from white women. A hunchback girl, coming across his poems, which express her own feeling of isolation, writes to him, and they begin a correspondence which becomes the chief interest and consolation of their lives. And so forth and so on. It's all extremely well-worked out and very poignant, but between lunch and tea I'm not at my most lyrical. So I'll pass on to Harris, who was much taken with the book, and asked Merrick and me to lunch at the Savoy. Merrick, then in his late forties, was a little man with large mournful eyes, shy but, like many shy people, stubborn. He insisted that *Conrad in Quest of His Youth* was his best novel, probably because the hero is pictured as quite a man of the world, with a taste in wine and a dash of the amorist. Harris, brushing *Conrad* aside, told Merrick that he found him in the hero of *The Quaint Companions*. The book was great stuff, he roared, though Merrick should have heated it with the negro's sensual appeal to the hero's mother. Merrick continued to be dogged about *Conrad*, and a little later maintained, against Harris, that most actresses were straight. 'I don't want straight women,' roared Harris. 'I want them with curves.' I have a very vivid picture of the two of them walking in front of me and another guest after we left the Savoy, Merrick short and slight, Harris short and broad, Harris booming and gesticulating, Merrick for the most part looking straight in front of him, with occasional jerks of his head in the direction from which the gale was blowing.

"A few weeks later Harris went over to France, and while there visited Merrick and his wife in their French home. On his return he said he had told Merrick that when he read *The Quaint Companions* he knew Merrick was either a cripple or a Jew.

"'How did Mrs. Merrick take that?', I asked.

"Pondering my question, which seemed to clarify some obscure impression Harris replied meditatively 'I believe she didn't like it.'

"To give Merrick a lift, I wrote about him in *Hearth and Home*, pointing out that the great themes, passion, hatred, revenge, and so on, were outside his range, but that his handling of slighter matters was admirable. He wrote and thanked me for my article in a letter which, at the time, I took to be a heartfelt tribute to my critical powers, but which I later realised to be faintly ironical, and indeed a most excellent example of the delicate talent I had allowed him to possess.''

TOMATO FARMS

After tea Trelawny showed the travellers over the house, taking them on to the roof, where they wondered at the huge chimney-stacks. ''Along that track,'' said Pearson, pointing to the road running west under the Chilterns, ''Shakespeare used to journey to and from Stratford whenever he didn't go by Oxford—whenever, in short, he felt that the chilliness of John Davenant's welcome would be more unpleasant than the warmth of Mrs. Davenant's would be the reverse.''

''Chequers is just over there,'' said Trelawny. ''In fact, Wellwick is the Dower House of Chequers, and Anthony Eden was attracted by it, but, as it happened, I'd already arranged to take it.''

They descended, and admired the house from the lawn, which was sheltered from the north-east by an old red-brick wall where fruit and flowers were trained. Two or three hundred yards to the south stood some ancient barns, and a profusion of haystacks, aesthetically too numerous, but, from the practical standpoint, no doubt just the right quantity. Trelawny took them over one of the barns, the immensity of which suggested to Pearson what a cathedral built by Anglo-Saxons would have been like, had they anticipated the Gothic style. Leaving the barn, they rambled in a northerly direction down a grassy avenue, along which Sir Edmunde Brudenell used to ride to church with his dame and children. The church bells were ringing as they turned home, passing a new-born calf which hobbled apprehensively to its mother, by whom it was comforted. "A reassuring lick," Trelawny murmured. In the last field before they reached home the sun, which had been hidden most of the day, shone through the distant clouds which stretched across the horizon like the Delectable Mountains. Before supper, Trelawny showed them the verses written by Sir Edmunde Brudenell on the death of four of his children—

> Cruell Death by Mortell Blades
> Hath Slain Foure of my tender Babes . . .
> O Dorothye my blessed Chylde
> Which lovingly lyved and dyed mylde
> Thou wert my tenth even Gods owne Choyse
> In Thee exceedingly I did rejoyse.

Kingsmill was puzzled by the "Mortell Blades," as Cromwell had not passed that way, and Trelawny said that he had pondered the phrase in vain. "Surely," remarked Pearson, "the meaning is obvious. The 'Mortell Blades' are simply Death's scythe. Brudenell wasn't Shakespeare, and, besides, he wanted what he thought was a rhyme for 'Babes.'" The other two having sat for a few moments with corrugated brows, Kingsmill sighed—"How moving the verses are." "Most," agreed Trelawny.

They had a very happy supper, during which everything went swimmingly, the travellers continuing to conform with Mrs. Irving's earlier wish that they should not complicate things by trying to help her. Prompted by Kingsmill, who had often told his host that if he would put his business adventures on paper they would be at least as absorbing as his great-grandfather's memoirs, Trelawny recounted the story of his first enterprise. In his youth he had gone to Paris as an art student, but soon noticed that the ratio of supply to demand was excessive, five thousand pictures being produced for every one that was sold. He returned to England, where he combined literature and the law. Here, too, there was more supply than demand; so when, during a holiday at Le Touquet, he saw an old fellow-student of Paris days in the Casino, looking very prosperous and gambling freely, he approached him in an inquiring frame of mind. His friend told him he had made a fortune out of mushrooms. Some years later, after a breakdown, he saw an advertisement asking for a sleeping partner in a tomato farm, and, remembering his mushroom friend, invested £250 in the farm. On receiving his first dividend of 15 per cent. he was so greatly encouraged that he persuaded some friends to join with him in buying a tomato farm at Basingstoke. No sooner was this transaction completed than the original tomato farm blew up, being a bogus concern which had been paying dividends out of capital. "Last year," Trelawny concluded, "my tomato farm at Basingstoke made a profit of £80,000."

"We all have our tomato farm," said Kingsmill sententiously. "Hesketh planted his under Beerbohm Tree." After a few protests, Pearson cleared his throat and thus began—

"The first part I ever played on the professional stage was Publius, an ancient senator in *Julius Caesar*, which Beer-

bohm Tree revived at his annual Shakespeare Festival in
1911. Publius was supposed to be the oldest politician in
Rome, and wishing to represent him as the oldest man on
earth, I made a close study of senility in the streets. At last
I got the quavering voice and tottering gait to a nicety, and
with the help of a white beard about a yard long and as
many wrinkles as I could paint on my face I felt equal to
the three words of my part, which consisted of 'Good-
morrow, Caesar.' When the moment came for my entrance
I was concentrating exclusively on the correct falsetto pitch
of my voice, and walked on the stage with the jaunty air
of the twenties instead of the palsied limp of six score.
Quickly realising my error, I paused to wonder whether it
would be possible to return to the wings and make an
entrance more appropriate to my beard and wrinkles; but
the actor who was playing the part of Caesar solved the
problem for me by saying 'Welcome, Publius,' which in
the text followed my 'Good-morrow, Caesar.' This floored
me, and I forgot to pipe the necessary words, saying instead,
quite distinctly and in my natural voice, 'Hullo!' Paralysed
by the catastrophe, I hobbled across the stage, tripped over
my toga and fell into the wings. I was prepared for the
sack, and was considering suicide when Tree came up to me
and asked what I had said to Caesar. In despair I blurted
out that I had said 'Hullo!' 'Oh. I beg your pardon. My
mistake. I thought you said "What ho!" ' remarked Tree,
who appeared to be grieved that I had not made the most of
the opportunity.

"After that it may seem strange that I was cast for the
part of Balthazar in *The Merchant of Venice*, which was
revived the following week; but I think I owed this to the
boisterous way in which I had spoken the line of a citizen

in the Forum scene of *Caesar*. In Tree's production Balthazar was played as a very dignified major-domo, and I
decided to model myself on my uncle's butler. He was a
very aloof kind of person, and in an attempt to find out
whether he was human I asked him one day what were his
private thoughts. 'If I told you my private thoughts, sir,
they would no longer be private,' he replied. As half a
dozen big productions were put on in as many weeks, the
rehearsals were scrappy, and I had not been told that a blast
of trumpets was the signal for my appearance, another blast
being heard before I opened my mouth. My cue came, and
I made a most impressive entrance with my wand of office.
My speech to Portia ran as follows: 'The four strangers
seek for you, madam, to take their leave, and there is a
forerunner come from a fifth, the Prince of Morocco, who
brings word the Prince his master will be here to-night.'
But just as I opened my mouth to deliver it, the first blast
of trumpets knocked me sideways. At its conclusion I
pulled myself together, and was about to make a second
attempt when the next blast shattered me and drove the
words out of my head. Silence restored, I gaped at Portia,
chary of speech. As Shakespeare had not foreseen the
occasion, but as something had to be done about it, she
prompted me with 'Well, sirrah?' I was quite equal to a
conversation on these lines. 'Well, madam?' I retorted.
Being unanswerable, this delayed the action of the scene.
Suddenly I heard the ferocious whisper of the stage-
manager: 'Get off the stage, you bloody idiot!' I did not
stop to argue."

The last train for London was at nine-eight, and the
travellers, after a regretful farewell to their hostess, were
motored by Trelawny to Wendover, the lights in the

valley below bringing home to them that the war really was over, and sending their minds back to the lights twinkling through the latticed windows in Barnsley nearly seven years before.

A BOSTON MINISTER

On Saturday, September 22, Pearson reached the Club with his knowledge of human nature increased, he said, by an incident he had observed on the way.

PEARSON: Coming along on the top of the bus I noticed a woman selling flags to two other women. The seller was being very sweet and charming, but after she'd closed the transaction and given a farewell smile to her customers, she looked up and, catching my eye, showed consciousness that she'd been behaving rather foolishly. From this trivial incident I glean the knowledge that when women put over an act on one another they do it self-consciously, when on men they do it intuitively.

KINGSMILL: She looked self-conscious because she'd been forcing geniality in order to sell a flag. If she'd been selling the flag to two men, and then caught the eye of a woman, she would no doubt have looked just as self-conscious as when she caught your eye. On the whole I agree with Harris that men and women are not "profoundly differenced."

PEARSON: Then he made a lot of fuss about very little, considering the amount of attention he gave to splitting the difference.

The weather being still unpropitious to movement, the travellers settled themselves down in their favourite corner. An American nearby, hearing someone address Kingsmill by name, came over and said how much he had enjoyed *Skye High*, whereupon Kingsmill presented Pearson as his partner on that enterprise. From a card produced by the American they learned he was the Rev. Russell Henry Stafford, Minister of the Old South Church in Boston. Declining an offer of a drink or lunch, he said that his nerves were in a pitiable condition over his prospective passage on the "Queen Mary." With a jovial smile he told them of the purgatory he had been going through. "First, I went on a visit of enquiry to Berkeley Square, vibrating like a violin string. A waste of time. Then other journeys. All useless. At last, by the pure chance of sitting at dinner next to a man who knew the right strings to pluck, I got a permit for a passage. Two years it's taken me! Actually, gentlemen, a week, but it seems like two years. And, gentlemen, if with this permit, countersigned by the British Government, I don't get on board, I'll finish what we started in 1776." Shaking hands warmly and swiftly, and assuring them of a hearty welcome in Boston, he rushed from the Club.

HAMPSTEAD HEATH

After lunch Douglas Jerrold joined them, and inquiring about the book received their assurance that, weather permitting, they would see what they could do for him after tea. Weather permitted, and they took the tube to

3, The Grove, Highgate, (Coleridge)

Highgate. Passing along the Grove they paused outside Coleridge's house, and Pearson pointed to The Flask Inn. "That," he said, "is where Hogarth broke a bottle over someone's head, or broke someone's head with a bottle—it doesn't matter which, at least to us—and where Carlyle, I take it, frequently dashed in for a double to drown the taste of Coleridge's bottled moonshine." Descending West Hill, they turned down towards Highgate Pond, and up along the lane where Keats met Coleridge. Pearson remembered it as a thoroughfare through the Kenwood Estate. In those days, he said, it was enclosed by palings, now it was a part of the heath. "But why are those iron railings round that pond?" he asked. "Is it to keep children from drowning themselves? If so, why?" Turning left, they went along the south edge of the Bois de Caen, which Pearson explained to Kingsmill was the original name for Kenwood, and doubtless given it by one of the Conqueror's knights, who was presumably a native of Caen in Normandy.

They rested for a while on a seat inscribed "In memory of May Orton A Lover of Hampstead," and looked at the far-off dome of St. Paul's—all of London that was visible between two groups of yellowing trees which faced one another at the far end of the heath.

"It would be worth leaving earth for heaven, if heaven turned out to be Hampstead Heath," ruminated Pearson, after a long pause. "By the way, that fine house up there with the white pillars against the red brick is where Harvey du Cros used to live, the big financier, for whom, as you may remember, Frank Harris wrote some political speeches, which, as later came out in court, du Cros did not value as highly as Frankie did."

"Yes," said Kingsmill, "I can see the old rascal on that terrace, with London at his feet, tugging at his mustachios and bellowing—'By Gard, du Cros, if I had your money I wouldn't stand for Parliament, I'd buy it, building and members, bricks and brainless boobies, and sink the bloody

lot in the Channel those God-damned sons of bitches down
there are pleased to call British.' ''

From Jack Straw's Castle they looked over towards
Harrow Hill, which was defined against the setting sun. A
rosy mist veiled the acres of little houses in Golders Green
and Hendon, turning the landscape once more into country,
as it had been in their early years.

MRS. DAVENANT AND HERMIONE

"I'm sure Mrs. Davenant is the original of Hermione in
The Winter's Tale," said Pearson during dinner at the
Club on Tuesday, September 25. "Shakespeare was often at
Oxford playing before the University after the great success
of *Hamlet* in 1602 or 3, and as Sir William Davenant, who
told Betterton and Samuel Butler that he was Shakespeare's
son, was born in 1606, it's clear that Shakespeare's affair
with Mrs. Davenant belonged to the period of the
Tragedies. William Davenant's putative father, John, was
a dour puritan, and all his children took after him except
William, who inherited Shakespeare's vivacity. I'm sure
both Desdemona and Hermione were drawn from Mrs.
Davenant. If they weren't central figures in tragedy they'd
be very serene and happy, as is obvious in the lighter scenes
Shakespeare is able to give them. What sweet, graceful,
lovable creatures they are!"

KINGSMILL: And I think one can add Imogen, who is in
exactly the same situation as Desdemona and Hermione.

By the way, it occurs to me that Mamillius may well have been suggested by young William Davenant, who would have been four or five when Shakespeare was writing *The Winter's Tale*. He's a very lifelike kid, with touches which seem to have been taken down on the spot.

PEARSON: And the situation in Leontes' household is roughly parallel to that in Davenant's. Leontes is a sour, crabbed fellow, even at his best, which doesn't last long, and so no doubt was the puritanical Davenant.

KINGSMILL: Perhaps Davenant's sourness with his wife is in *Cymbeline*, too, when Imogen complains 'And I shall here abide the hourly shot of angry eyes.' But Leontes–Hermione is a closer parallel to Mr. and Mrs. Davenant than Posthumus–Imogen; and Shakespeare easily slipped into the part of Polixenes, who is supposed to be a carefree youth in the twenties and yet says of his son that with 'his varying childness he cures in me thoughts that would thick my blood'–Shakespeare in the middle forties.

PEARSON: And, like Polixenes, Shakespeare must often have felt in Davenant's household 'Methinks my favour here begins to warp.' And I daresay Davenant, like Leontes, occasionally tried to make Shakespeare feel at home, and Mrs. Davenant, like Hermione, sat by tongue-tied.

KINGSMILL: Of course, Shakespeare also slipped quite easily into the part of Leontes, and so Leontes expresses not what Davenant felt about Mrs. Davenant, but what he himself had felt about the Black Mistress of the Sonnets. Hence the fantastic way in which Leontes carries on, which is simply Shakespeare's retrospective rage, and the completely unconvincing poltroonery of Polixenes, who runs the moment he sees the red light. As he has nothing on his conscience so far as Hermione is concerned, there is no reason why he should not ask Leontes why he is behaving so oddly. But at this point of the play Shakespeare is interested only in Leontes' feelings, and merely wants to get Polixenes out of the way.

PEARSON: What a pity we can't have Hermione's view of both of them!

KINGSMILL: In the form of a diary, you mean? Let us try.

PEARSON: 'Monday. Leo's old school friend, Polixenes, has arrived. I do hope the visit will be a success.'

KINGSMILL: 'Tuesday. Leo and his friend have been hunting to-day. I do hope the exercise will have done Leo good. He goes out so seldom.'

PEARSON: 'Wednesday. I was busy all day over the play and banquet. I think Leo enjoyed them. He does need to be taken out of himself at present.'

KINGSMILL: 'Thursday. A quiet day. Leo had a headache, so I had to amuse Polixenes. Fortunately he was quite ready to talk about himself.'

PEARSON: 'Friday. Leo has been queer all day. He seemed to be muttering to himself. I do hope it's only a passing indisposition. Thank goodness, Polixenes never seems to notice anything.'

KINGSMILL: 'Saturday. Polixenes left after lunch without saying good-bye. I saw him running down to the harbour with his attaché case and his hat pulled over his eyes. And a few minutes later a speed-boat disappeared round the headland. I do wish Leo had a really sensible friend.'

RICHMOND

Over lunch at the Club on Saturday, September 29, Pearson regretted that Shakespeare's connection with Court circles prevented him from being as unpleasant about men of action as he obviously longed to be.

KINGSMILL: His longing to be unpleasant isn't very obvious when he says of Mark Antony 'A rarer spirit never did steer humanity.'

PEARSON: He was thinking of himself, not Antony.

KINGSMILL: Even so, I don't see that one gains much by substituting Shakespeare, who wasn't steering in any direction, for Mark Antony, who was steering in the wrong one.

Looking out of the window, Kingsmill sighed—"It's a glorious day—unfortunately. Well, where shall it be?"

"The easiest place to get to from here is Richmond—three hundred yards to the underground."

"Then Richmond let it be."

On the way out of Richmond Station a man at least four inches taller than Pearson collided with him and hurried on, quite unimpaired as it seemed to Kingsmill. Pearson, looking after the man rather balefully, muttered "I nearly knocked that fellow down as he passed. . . . What the hell are you laughing at?"

As they walked along the main street, Kingsmill said that it looked as unprepossessing as when he used to come down

Gateway, Richmond Palace

63

thirty years ago on the way to Twickenham. "If there's anything beautiful in or near Richmond, I've quite forgotten it," he added. "I haven't," said Pearson briskly, "and so this higgledy-piggledy thoroughfare doesn't worry me. We turn down here to the Green."

They came out on the wide expanse of Richmond Green. It was a bright autumn afternoon, and as they looked about them they agreed that it was the best day since Cockfosters, Kingsmill adding that Douglas might think it the only one. "There," said Pearson, "is where Kean's Theatre used to stand. Those houses range from Queen Anne to William IV. Those, on the other hand, as you presumably perceive, are mid-Victorian, but not too bad in this setting. We will now cross the Green, and I will show you a very beautiful terrace. . . . This was originally an enormous country mansion built in the time of William and Mary. Now, as you may notice, it is split up. In those days people didn't build houses for gentlemen contiguous to one another. Now, as those dividing walls show, the place has been parcelled out in a number of residences. But, except for those partitions, it's all exactly as it was—those railings, for example, and those old balls." "Of which we have now had enough," said Kingsmill firmly.

They passed through the arch of the ancient Palace, and Pearson, reviving, said "There's the wing in which Shakespeare and his troupe must have stayed when they played before Queen Elizabeth just before her death."

KINGSMILL: Nowadays I often find myself, when looking at an old building like this, thinking how strange it is that those bricks have been there, completely motionless, year after year, with everything rising and falling, appearing and vanishing, round them.

PEARSON: All the raving and roaring and howling and groaning in the world since they were first placed there.

KINGSMILL: All the ideas that have been put forward.

PEARSON: And all the ideas that have been put back.

KINGSMILL: And what comes home to me even more strongly is that those bricks haven't shifted, not by one inch, since my own appearance on the scene.

PEARSON: That bit of mortar there—not batted an eyelid— while I . . . while I . . .

KINGSMILL: It's consoling in a way. One likes to think they were there on such and such a day in the past. It seems to fix that moment and lift it out of time.

Pearson breathed again, and they walked down to the tow path. As they were strolling along by the river (towards Petersham Common, Pearson said), two pretty young girls smiled tentatively at Kingsmill, who, wondering if it were an optical illusion, turned round. They had turned too, and were still smiling. "Isn't it Mr. Kingsmill?" one of them said, and he remembered they had been friends of his son Tony at Hastings. After giving them all the information in his power, he proceeded thoughtfully towards Pearson, who was standing some distance up the tow path, gravely regarding a fisherman. "Although I believe in immortality," said Kingsmill, as they continued on their way, "there are times when one feels rather more mortal than at others."

"Testing. Very testing," sighed Pearson.

They climbed the hill, and sat down on the terrace.

KINGSMILL: This is Turner's view, isn't it? It doesn't look as spacious as in Turner's picture. Are we facing west?

PEARSON: Yes (*jabbing his finger west, north, east and south*).

KINGSMILL: I always like looking west. In fact, now that you tell me we are looking west, the landscape is opening out a bit.

PEARSON: I've just had a revelation. Humanity is always talking about the dawn and is always travelling towards the sunset, which shows that it doesn't believe in the dawn, and indeed is running away from it.

Going on a little farther, they came to what really was Turner's view, and saw the shining river dividing round a thickly wooded island.

As they went on towards the Park, they passed a pram which was standing on a slope. Noticing that the baby's feet were higher than its head, Kingsmill exclaimed in some agitation "I don't think it's good for the baby. Oughtn't we to say something to the mother?", but Pearson dismissed the suggestion with "Far be it from me to dictate to a mother how to murder her own child." Kingsmill, enchanted by the huge old trees in the Park and the expanse of rolling green beyond, asked his friend how far the Park stretched. "About four miles straight on and about two and a half across. Robin Hood Gate is three miles from where we're sitting, and beyond that lies Wimbledon Common. Putney is *there*–Kingston is *there*–and Hampton Court is *there.*"

Returning along the terrace, they descended Richmond Hill, and had tea in the British India Restaurant, an eighteenth-century building which, they noticed, provided curry and other Oriental dishes, and seemed the kind of place in which Colonel Newcome, tired of his Bayswater relatives, would have smoked a cheroot and with a sigh remembered old days in Bengal.

In order to avoid returning to the station by the main

street, they diverged to the right along Ormond Road, and at once found themselves in the eighteenth century. It was only of late years, said Kingsmill, that he had begun to realise how much of the past still lingered in England. "When I was young, I had a vague feeling that everything had been run up about ten years back, and that the past was irretrievably gone. Now in 1945 I'm constantly in or about 1745. But perhaps you will help me to be a little more precise." "That," said Pearson, coming to a halt, "is a Georgian bow window superimposed on a William and Mary house—a sign of increasing wealth. Belloc and all the Black Death Merry Englanders to the contrary, and notwithstanding the enthusiasts for the spacious and plague-smitten days of great Elizabeth, the England we know, and the England best worth knowing, is the England which began with Dutch William. Look at those warm red-brick houses, homely yet stately—they seem to be saying, 'We've come through all this, and now we're here and we're here to stay.'"

Turning into Church Terrace, they were brought back to the twentieth century by a placard on a Queen Anne house bearing the words OUR DUMB FRIEND'S LEAGUE—RECEIVING SHELTER FOR CATS.

"A headache for Hogarth, that," murmured Pearson. "But I'm glad of it."

In the close surrounding Richmond Parish Church, in which, Kingsmill agreed with Pearson, Kean was buried, a house caught their eye. It stood in a little verandahed court-yard and had a nautical look, as though it had been fitted together out of the sides of a ship which had fought at Trafalgar. The evening sun mellowed it, and the travellers returned once more to the past.

INDICATIVE

The first fortnight of October, a period of unbroken fine
weather, indeed an Indian summer which even the
remembrance of septuagenarians could not, in Shakespeare's
unintelligible jargon, parallel a fellow to, Pearson went on
holiday in Cornwall with his friend James Mitchell. When
he and Kingsmill met once more on October 20, the weather
was again unfriendly to outdoor enterprise, and the
travellers passed the day in the Club. Asked by Kingsmill
how he had enjoyed his Cornish ramble, Pearson said that
he had taken advantage of the fine weather to sit and sleep
in the sun, occasionally reaching for the George Saintsbury
Memorial Volume.

PEARSON: I don't know why, but I've always been
interested in Saintsbury. If I ever see his name in an index,
I invariably turn up the reference. It isn't that he's
personally interesting, but he had a real eye for what's
interesting in other men's work. Also, his odd jerky
parenthetical style attracts me. He seems perpetually to be
on the verge of a disclosure which, if made, would jar on
his academic propriety.

KINGSMILL: A don always about to burst into tears and
confess that he is a human being after all.

PEARSON: Of course one doesn't *look* for his name in an
index. The names I personally look for are Shakespeare,
first, and then Johnson and Boswell, Sydney Smith,
Wellington, Beethoven, Cromwell and Carlyle, and, if the
book is a recent one, Wilde and Shaw and Harris.

KINGSMILL: My choice is more or less the same, but I
would add Balzac, Wordsworth and Goethe. However, I
often find God instead of Goethe.

68

PEARSON: That serves you right. But you know my opinion of both.

READING MATTER

Pearson, who had with him a recent volume in the World's Classics, *Specimens of English Dramatic Criticism*, asked Kingsmill whether he had ever realised that both Shaw and Hazlitt hated the theatre. He had not, said Kingsmill. "The editor of this volume," Pearson continued, "states it as a fact, unaware that some of the happiest hours of Hazlitt's life were spent in a particular seat at Covent Garden, and that Shaw used to devote every possible sixpence to the pit or gallery of any theatre. He also writes 'We have no evidence that Shakespeare cared a jot about his plays as reading matter.' This statement is in flat contradiction of Shakespeare's revised will. After making the first draft, he realised he was too ill to prepare his own works for the press, and asked Heming and Condell to do it for him; and in the revised will leaves them memorial rings in token of his gratitude for their agreement to do so. Further, he left a ring to Richard Burbage, who knew the plays better than anyone except Shakespeare himself, and was therefore the one man to help out Heming and Condell wherever the text was obscure. This isn't supposition, it's simply what Heming and Condell say in the Preface to the first Folio, interpreted in the light of the revised will. Why should Shakespeare, alone of great writers, be supposed to be utterly indifferent to fame,

69

he who opened his dramatic career with 'Let fame, that all hunt after in their lives . . .'?"

KINGSMILL: I've noticed that the people who argue that Shakespeare was superior to the desire to be remembered for his writing think it perfectly natural and proper that he should have done his best to strengthen his rather shaky position as a country gentleman by entailing his estate on his male issue. It is the old levelling instinct. Bad enough that Shakespeare should have written masterpieces, but if he didn't realise it, that's something, and if he wanted his grandchildren to be more gentlemanly than himself, that's something more.

Before parting, Pearson suggested to Kingsmill that they should go out to Ayot St. Lawrence and visit Bernard Shaw. Kingsmill said it would be delightful. He had, he said, seen Shaw on behalf of Frank Harris, on behalf of Robert Harborough Sherard, and on behalf of himself, and would now be glad to see him in his own interests. So it was agreed that Pearson should write to Shaw and propose a visit. "One thing I would like to find out," said Kingsmill, "is whether his prejudice against Thackeray owed anything to his association with Edmund Yates. Yates may have given him his version of his trouble with Thackeray, and Shaw has always been very nice about his editors, as one knows in the test case of Frank Harris."

On the afternoon of Friday, October 26, pursuant to their policy of treating Southern England as London, Kingsmill joined Pearson and James Mitchell at Charing Cross for a long week-end at Battle. As the train started, he said that it was just possible, though most unlikely, that his wife would be ringing him up that evening with news about his brother Brian, which would necessitate his return to town. Pearson having expressed concern, and Mitchell having, with Scotch caution, inclined his head non-committally, Kingsmill continued: "You have had experience of Brian's incalculable ways, Hesketh. Well, he's at it again. He's been in Italy and Austria for some months with U.N.R.R.A., but the day before yesterday, when I was at *Punch*, I suddenly heard his measured tone on the telephone telling me that he had left Vienna that morning—on foot, to judge from his unhurried utterance—and could we meet the following day? We arranged to have an early tea at the Kardomah yesterday, but just as I was leaving the office to meet him, Miss Williams, the editor's secretary, told me, rather breathlessly, that a lady had rung up while I was at lunch to say that my brother was out of danger and was expected to live. Which brother? I asked. But Miss Williams had no information on this point; so after ringing up Arnold and gathering that he was expecting to die, but not at present, I did not see what further steps I could take, Brian not having given me any address."

"And you are leaving London with your brother in a critical condition?" inquired Mitchell severely.

"Well, Miss Williams said that this lady, who is no doubt Belinda, Brian's future wife, would ring me up in the evening. So, as she didn't, I presume Brian is, as indeed she herself said, out of danger and expected to live."

"You presume a great deal on insufficient evidence, Hughie," said Mitchell.

"My own belief is that Brian has had one of his attacks, and that Belinda, who isn't accustomed to them, has naturally been very much alarmed. These attacks are a kind of clearing-house. They do Brian good and, in their secondary aspect, render everyone round him apprehensive and malleable. I imagine he wants to be in England to preside over the publication of his autobiography. That's only natural; it's a fascinating book and as original as Brian himself. But he might feel that leaving his job in Vienna would come in for a certain amount of criticism from his family, and this is his way of numbing it."

"You've thought that all out very carefully," said Mitchell, "and I hope your conscience will remain stupefied during this holiday which you're so determined to have, come what may to everyone except yourself."

Kingsmill turned to Pearson, who obligingly gave him the moral support he stood in need of; and opening their papers the travellers relapsed into silence.

Dinner when they arrived at the George Hotel was postponed for over an hour while Pearson, drinking ale with three friends, absorbed all the rural happenings since he had left Whatlington in the summer; Mitchell, an old visitor at the George, co-operating in a cordial and acquiescent humour, Kingsmill sitting near the door, peevish and hungry.

In the lounge after dinner Kingsmill picked up *The Times*, which had a headline "Oxford Degrees for Service Leaders," and photographs of Generals Eisenhower and

Mark Clark, Bernard Freyburg and Montgomery. "I don't quite understand," he said, "why men of blood and iron should, after they have shed a satisfactory amount of blood and used up a reasonable quota of iron, be singled out as experts in Law and Letters. But I don't want to be captious, and would be quite satisfied if the compliment were returned—for example, Lord Simon, V.C., and General Bernard Shaw and Admiral T. S. Eliot and Sibelius, D.S.O."

"And I suppose Hot-Air Marshal Hugh Kingsmill?" said Mitchell.

THE BATTLE

Kingsmill, although he had lived so long at Hastings and had so frequently visited Battle, had never seen the site where the battle was fought. So on the following evening Pearson took him on a tour of inspection. Starting from the main gate of the Abbey, they went down a path which skirted the Abbey grounds, passing by trees some of which looked as if they had been there in 1066, and others as though they had sprung from the acorns showered down during the fight.

KINGSMILL: This is just the silence and rustle of incipient dusk which Carlyle speaks of when he rode over here from St. Leonards.

PEARSON: There's the hill on which Duke William raised his standard. The Saxons were up there, and they had a bloody encounter down here in this valley–the most important moment in history, for those lads were engaged in creating the conditions in which the world's finest poetry, greatest humour and richest wit could be produced. Here, in short, is the breeding-ground of Shakespeare and Johnson, of Wordsworth and Sydney Smith.

KINGSMILL: Though one may read Belloc for the Normans and Freeman and Stubbs for the Saxons without getting any inkling of what the battle was about.

They went on through the quiet fields, occasionally starting slightly as a massive shape oscillated in the dusk and emitted a sound of champing. But on the whole they kept themselves well in hand as they crossed the zone of conflict.

THE SWEETNESS OF COLIN HURRY

Colin Hurry was coming down for lunch on Sunday, and while waiting for him, Kingsmill said to Pearson, "It must be nearly thirty years since you were in Persia with Colin. I suppose you're his oldest friend."

MITCHELL: Ill-informed as usual, my boy. I knew Colin seven years before Hesketh did.

KINGSMILL: Good staying power in Colin. Where did you meet him?

MITCHELL: He met me at Liverpool. We were in Lever Brothers together.

KINGSMILL: I wish I could visualise Colin's transit

through the world of finance. I always think of him and Trelawny as the poets in King Midas's Court, but the difficulty is to get them to offer their masterpieces for lay inspection.

PEARSON: Colin is strangely detached, and I sometimes wonder whether he thinks writers or business men the bigger fools, but he's so sweet-natured that he's managed to keep his secret.

Over lunch, Kingsmill having suggested that there was great need for a corps of Social Commandos, picked men who would attend public functions for the purpose of spreading alarm and despondency and bringing the proceedings into ridicule and contempt, Colin Hurry said he believed he had some qualifications for the job, and proceeded:—

"I was at a big lunch the other day. I needn't tell you what it was in aid of, and in any case I can't remember. The main thing, indeed the only thing which interested those present, was the excellence of the lunch. Opposite me was a bland cleric, and next to him a dignified old gentleman who listened to him with a courtesy which hardly concealed his intense boredom. Suddenly the cleric leant across and addressed me as follows—'We are having a very serious conversation this side of the table. We are discussing the reason for the emptiness of the churches.' 'That's easy,' I replied. 'The priests of Christ no longer practise Christianity.' 'I know very humble and devoted priests,' he said, 'whose churches nevertheless are empty.' 'Perhaps because they carry Christianity into the homes of the people, and don't expect a return visit.' 'Well, *my* church isn't empty,' he retorted, naming it. The name was familiar to me, and I replied 'That's easy. This is the age of

75

bread and circuses, and you're part of the circus.' He looked rather hurt, but replied with patient dignity 'I fully realise it is to better men than myself that I owe my congregations.'

" 'They realise it, too. By the way, what are you doing here?'

" 'I was invited.'

" 'Yes, but why did you accept the invitation? After all, what is this occasion? I'm eating the rations of a family for two days. Being a sinner, that comes naturally to me; but what about you? Your being here is incomprehensible to me. This consorting with publicans and sinners was never meant to stop short at gorging and swilling with them.' At this point I noticed the old gentleman gazing at me rather sadly, with a kind of *O tempora! O mores!* look in his eye.

"One of my anti-clerical days, I'm afraid."

After lunch Kingsmill took his son, Brooke, who had come over from his school, into Hastings, preceded a little earlier by Pearson and Colin. On reaching Hastings, Pearson and Colin stood for some time watching the sea dashing over the breakwater by the fishing village; and Colin was inspired to complete a quatrain that had been running in his head on the journey from London.

October 28, 1945.

"Words, Words, Words",

In the beginning Chaos, then the Word.
Then light; and life upon the Planet stirred.
Now, aeons after, Chaos rules again.
The Word forgotten, only words remain.

They found Kingsmill and his son on the bus for Battle. The afternoon had been wet and dismal, and both of them were rather listless. Pearson asked Brooke if he collected bus tickets and, hearing that he did, handed him a ten-shilling note. "It's been worth coming, after all," said Brooke. As the elders got off at Battle, Colin slipped Brooke another note, and the last they saw of him was a satisfied smile.

"GOD'S ACRE" JAMIE

Monday was fine, and after breakfast Kingsmill accompanied Mitchell on his regular morning pilgrimage round the church. Under the spell of this peculiarly beautiful God's Acre, from which the fields sloped down to a group of old farm buildings and rose beyond to a distant tree-lined horizon, the obdurate Scot became tractable and gentle, putting Kingsmill right barely six times in the course of their amiable perambulation. "I shall try to remember you like this in future," said Kingsmill. "For me you are henceforth 'God's Acre' Jamie. Sorry, but there it is." "Don't apologise. It's I should be sorry that I can't benefit from a corresponding change in yourself."

OLD HASTINGS

Leaving Kingsmill at his work on Monday morning, the other three went over to see Mr. Bertram Dodd, who kept the inn at John's Cross, where, Pearson told them, they would receive the heartiest welcome and drink the best beer in England.

In the afternoon all four motored over to Hastings, but, when the question of dismounting and walking along the front arose, Mitchell decided to return to Battle and send back the car. It was a clear, bright afternoon. As they walked towards the East Cliff, the sea breaking in the sun and the old Regency houses to their left, and the shore now almost wholly free from the various objects and devices which it had been hoped would embarrass the enemy, it seemed as if the war were really over at last. They turned up into the old town, mouldering signboards creaking as they passed, and smugglers armed with cutlasses lurking in the dark and dangerous alleys.

Repressing, in deference to his companions, the numerous associations the East Cliff had for him, Kingsmill showed them the quickest way up, which they were careful not to follow. The ascent, completed in under five minutes, seemed to have raised them to a great height from which they looked down on the blue smoke swirling above the gully of the old town, and over at the white houses glistening on the West Cliff and the wooded hills to the north, and across the sea to Beachy Head, towards which the sun was declining.

DAWN

Waking at dawn the following day, Colin looked out of his window at the back of the George. The fields were covered in a mist which did not lie there inertly but seemed to be quivering with life. Two black spots jutted up through it, so spaced that together with himself they formed a triangle. Presently they defined themselves as a tree and a hill, the sun suddenly picked out a little white farmhouse, and the rest of the land rose up through the mist.

Colin and Kingsmill breakfasted early, and left for the station after telling Mr. Bristow, their courteous landlord, that they meant to return soon and often, and once again thanking Miss Grace Price, who had specially risen to give them breakfast, for her care and kindliness.

The compartment on the way up was crowded, and from Tunbridge Wells onwards two strident women churned occasional looks of anguish out of Colin and Kingsmill, who were facing one another.

"Hard, after your dawn?" murmured Kingsmill.

"Ah, that was really life," sighed Colin.

Meanwhile Mitchell and Pearson dressed, bathed and breakfasted at their leisure, idled through the day, and bestirred themselves only on the arrival of some friends, with whom they passed a boisterous evening, returning to London the next day by a late train in a compartment which they had to themselves.

CONAL O'RIORDAN

Having arranged to take tea with Conal O'Riordan on Friday, November 2, Pearson and Kingsmill walked to Netherlands House. On the way Kingsmill said that he had been right about Brian, so far as the attack went, but could not claim to have foreseen its setting. "A few hours after he'd rung me up at *Punch*, he went to the London Library, where Belinda was to meet him shortly before five. On arriving she found him prone beneath a white sheet. How he got there he does not know, and I do not propose to enquire of the attendants. Suffice it that he'd had a fit, and that it had fallen to them to suspend their usual duties in order to make him as comfortable as possible. The sheet was perhaps less for his sake than for that of their routine members. He did actually turn up at the Kardomah the next day, soon after I'd left, but as I'd just been told he was out of danger, it naturally didn't occur to me that he was also out of doors."

Introducing Pearson to Conal O'Riordan, whom he had known for many years, Kingsmill said how much it had interested him to read in a recent life of Ernest Dowson that Conal and he had walked through Flanders together in the 'nineties.

"We loved the carillon at Bruges," said O'Riordan, "and expected something as beautiful at Ypres, which, as you know, is another of those wonderful old Flemish towns. We were both agog for the first note of the chimes, and stood at our window looking down on the town square. Presently the steady tramp of a regiment was heard, and as they entered the square the bells feebly tinkled out a soldiers' march, like a worn-out musical box. I'm afraid that is the memory which has lasted longest with me, but I was very fond of Ernest, and he was just the gentle creature described by everyone who knew him."

Prompted by Kingsmill, O'Riordan told them some of his experiences in his Dublin years. He had been the first member of the Citizen Army enrolled by James Connolly, whom the English shot after the Easter rising. "Indeed," said O'Riordan, "I was not only the first member but the only one present on the first parade. But I wanted the Army to remain constitutional." He had, he said, been one of the Abbey Theatre group in its great days, and had produced Synge's *The Tinker's Wedding*. Asked by Kingsmill if Yeats had had much personal affection for Synge, O'Riordan smiled and said that Yeats's obituary notice of Synge had been written in very sonorous prose. "I was present," he said, "at a dinner to promote the theatre we were planning. A. P. Graves was in the chair; his brother wrote *Father O'Flynn*, you know, but A. P. hadn't much fun in him at all. And Yeats was no favourite of his, either, and I remember his expression when Yeats, at his most hierophantic, declaimed 'We don't wish merely for a theatre here in Dublin, for a building, but for rhapsodists pouring over the land.'

"At another dinner, I recall, A. P. Graves was talking to the Lord Chief Justice, and I asked him the way to the lavatory. 'Can't you see I'm talking to the Lord Chief Justice?' he said. 'I can,' I said, 'but I don't think he would object to your telling me where the lavatory is.'"

"I'm afraid," said Pearson to O'Riordan, who had just been through the manuscript of his Life of Wilde, "that Wilde doesn't appeal to you much?" O'Riordan detailed some of the reasons why he was out of sympathy with Wilde, and Robert Sherard being mentioned, said he had known him well. Indeed, on one occasion Sherard, who was a moody creature, came round and said he must shoot himself and wanted two pounds for a revolver. "It's lucky you came to me," O'Riordan told him, "for I've got a revolver, and you can have it."

"Well, I'm very glad he didn't avail himself of the offer," said Kingsmill, "for Hesketh and I had some very pleasant hours with him in his later and calmer years, and a great deal of fun and instruction out of his heroic support of Oscar Wilde against the united machinations of Frank Harris and Bernard Shaw."

As they walked back to the club, Pearson said he quite understood why O'Riordan did not take to Sherard—"He's the real fighting Anglo-Irishman, and reminds me of the Duke of Wellington, except when he smiles, and I daresay that held good for the Duke, too."

BULLS-EYES

At the Authors Club they were reminded not of Wellington but of Genghis Khan. Brian was in the bar with Malcolm Muggeridge, and his resonant tones came out to them as they drew near. "He's in one of his dynamic moods," murmured Kingsmill. "We're for it."

Promptly shaking Brian by the hand, Pearson said how glad he was that he had managed to escape from Vienna. Brian nodded, and turning to Muggeridge continued "I saw a lot of her in Vienna."

"Of whom?" asked Kingsmill.

"Stalin's daughter. She's a very cultivated woman, Malcolm. She's artistic and knows several languages."

"Are you sure it was Stalin's daughter?" asked Kingsmill. "I understand she plays Chopin on the pianola when Stalin wants to remember the dear, dead days and friends who have long gone silent. But the papers have left it at that."

"It was Krassin's daughter," said Brian, after a slight pause for reflection. Turning again to Muggeridge, whose scant sympathy for Soviet Russia was beginning to show in his expression, Brian continued "I've brought back a book I want to translate—a concise favourable account of the Soviet System."

Wishing to deflect Brian from Muggeridge before it was too late, Kingsmill interjected "If it's favourable, it must be concise."

Swivelling slowly round towards his brother, a tankard raised in one hand and a book in the other, Brian fixed him with his eyes and said "This is Gerhardi's autobiography. Now that I've written my own, I can read William's with equanimity." There was a full-fraught silence, during which Brian gazed at his brother as though conveying that if Kingsmill should ever write an autobiography he would read that with equanimity, too. As he turned back towards Muggeridge he caught sight of Pearson, who was on a high chair by the bar, smiling with gentle relish. "Oh, Hesketh!" he called out, "you'll be interested in this. Corti's brother, whom I saw a lot of in Vienna, has invented an entirely new form of biography. It's going to supersede all the old methods of writing biography. He explained it to me and I was greatly impressed. I'm seeing a publisher about it." He drained his tankard and placing it on the mantelpiece said "But I must go now, Belinda's waiting for me."

His voice came to them from the corridor, where he was telling Arthur Dawe that he was back from Vienna and had given up administrative work as he wished to devote himself entirely to literature.

TOWARDS HAMPTON COURT

After lunch at the Club on Saturday, November 3, Pearson and Kingsmill set out for Hampton Court, which it had been Kingsmill's fixed intention to visit since shortly after the close of the last war. In 1922 he had corresponded on the subject with Kenneth Hare, and in 1936 Pearson had made full arrangements to take him and Muggeridge there, ordering a car and booking a table for dinner at the local hostelry, and raining down curses on both of them after they had failed, for reasons which seemed to him inadequate, to turn up. But now at last he and Kingsmill were on the way. As they were crossing Hungerford Bridge they paused to take in the view of the curving river and St. Paul's. "Earth," said Pearson, "hath not anything to show more fair than the view from Westminster Bridge, according to Wordsworth. He was mistaken. It hath . . . from here. I like that old brewery, too," he continued, pointing to a building at the Surrey end of the bridge. "That red-brick lion, probably put there about 1830, is one of London's chief landmarks, but, perhaps because it's on a brewery and the wrong side of the river, no one mentions it. Yet it has been looked at in moments of depression and exaltation, terror, personal optimism, political apprehension, economic disquiet and amorous frenzy by, among others, Macaulay and Florence Nightingale, Mrs. Beeton and Dickens, Gladstone, Disraeli and Max Beerbohm, Major Attlee, you and me.''

"It's getting on for three," said Kingsmill, "the weather's not quite what I'd like, and it will be dark in a couple of hours. Do you think . . . ? Is it wise . . . ?''

"Very reckless," said Pearson. "I suggest the Tower instead.''

Retracing their steps, they entered the Underground and emerged at the Monument. As they walked through Billingsgate Market, the problems involved in collecting and distributing fish weighed on Kingsmill, the sense of Nottingham and the West Country waiting for deliveries, the checking here, the book-keeping there. "One wants a word to sum it all up and get rid of it," he exclaimed. "Piscatorial," snapped Pearson. "Thank you—something in the Carlyle vein perhaps?—'Piscatorial affairs thriving right well, I judge.' '' "That's got it," said Pearson. "By the way, there's the Custom House. When I was twenty I used to go in there with specifications and things like that.''

"Things like what?''

"Specifications.''

They turned up to Eastcheap, and emerging near Mincing Lane were exhilarated by the open spaces where they remembered rows of offices. Feeling a little light-headed, they turned to a passing dustman to find out if he shared their enthusiasm. He seemed more concerned for the beautiful buildings which had vanished together with the business premises. Pointing to the remains of the Parish

Church of St. Olave's in Park Street, which the disappearance of the intervening buildings made visible, he
said "That was a lovely old church, gold-fish in the garden
and all that."

As they went up Mincing Lane, Pearson gave a view-
halloo as he caught sight of Fenchurch Street Station,
which looked demure, as though not wishing to insist on
the fact that in being visible to people in Mincing Lane
it was exceeding what could legitimately be asked of it.
They passed by St. Olave's, where there were no signs of
goldfish, and reaching a gentle declivity, paused. "This,"
said Pearson, "is Tower Hill. Many necks have been
broken here—not, as you will observe, through plunging
over precipices, but by the executioner's axe; and of late
years it has been a convenient pitch for incendiary speeches
to strikers. Shaw used to orate here a good deal at one
time." "These fashionable Irish dramatists," said Kingsmill, "have a flair for the right mob to address, the House
of Commons for Sheridan when the upper classes counted,
Tower Hill for Shaw when the lower classes began to
count."

They entered the porch of All Hallow's Church, Barking,
and found three children there, who for Pearson's benefit
turned on a light which illuminated a model of the Toc H
Church at Poperinghe. On being offered some money by
Pearson, they refused after much head-shaking, whereupon,
perceiving that the incident was closed, he went out into
the street. Kingsmill put a shilling on a ledge and said
"Perhaps you can take this when we're gone," and heard a
rush of feet behind him as he joined Pearson. "Why
did those little blighters jib at the cash?" Pearson asked,
and learnt with amazement from Kingsmill that there were

86

wicked men in the world, and that children were warned by their mothers to be very careful with strangers.

They walked through the gardens skirting the enormous moat to the north of the Tower, and came to Tower Bridge. Noting that it had been opened in June 1894, Kingsmill said "It must have been that summer that my nurse took Arnold and me to see it. No doubt it was the sensation of the year; and I remember the Tower, the impression it made on me giving substance later to Harrison Ainsworth and generally filling out my romantic vision of the unromantic past. It is strange to think that day is a seventh of the way back from now to Shakespeare. The older one grows the nearer one gets to the past. When I was twenty I was about fifteen lives from Shakespeare. If I live to be a hundred, I shall be less than four."

"And if you live to be four hundred—or should it be three?—you'll be one of his contemporaries."

"Y–yes."

They scanned the Gothic Towers for signs of the mechanism which operated the pair of drawbridges; but seeing nothing to their purpose, rested their arms on the parapet and looked up-stream towards London Bridge. Clouds towered over the river and the City, half foreboding, half beautiful. To their right was Traitor's Gate, and they pictured Princess Elizabeth getting out of the boat there and wondering whether her sister Mary would ever let her get into it again.

Bernard Shaw having accepted their invitation to go and see him, Pearson and Kingsmill set forth by car after lunch on Monday, November 5. On the way Pearson said that the last time he had been to Ayot Shaw told him of a public speech he had once made in his native town of Dublin. It was to the Gaelic League, the members of which he irritated by saying that he wrote in a language understood by at least 300 million people in preference to one that could only be read by at most 3 million. There was a great deal of heckling, and at last he said "If you won't listen to me quietly, I'll make the rest of my speech in Gaelic, and not one of you will understand a syllable of it," and, he concluded, the calm of death descended upon them.

Kingsmill was greatly impressed by the size of Hatfield Park, and said it showed how much the spirit of the Conqueror and his knights still prevailed in Cecil's England that one man should have been able to engross so much of the public land to his own benefit. Meanwhile Pearson was looking out for a turning which led down to Ayot St. Lawrence, and, thinking he had passed it, asked the driver if he knew his way to Ayot. "Oh, yes," said the driver. "A very big gentleman lives there." Soon the car diverged to the left, and began, like a ferret after a venerable rabbit, to burrow through narrow country lanes, the high hedges on each side brushing it as it passed, on and on and on till Kingsmill at last exclaimed that Gray's Country Churchyard was Piccadilly Circus to this. As they stopped before the house, Pearson said "Don't forget to find out if Shaw's dislike of Thackeray was in any way due to Edmund Yates." Kingsmill nodded.

They were shown into the drawing-room, from which they looked down on a lawn, some rough ground planted with trees dipping beyond it, and fields rising on the other side of the hollow. From where they stood they could see Shaw reposing in the bay-window of the dining-room, and noted no very precipitate eagerness to rise and join them. At last he stirred, and coming into the drawing-room asked them to seat themselves.

PEARSON: How are you?

SHAW: Ninety.

PEARSON: Yes, but how are you feeling?

SHAW: Well, how does anyone feel at ninety? You'll know when you get there. I'm all right here at home, but it's troublesome in London, and if I fell down there, I might be picked up by a policeman and run in for being drunk. (*To H. K.*) By the way, I want you to tell me something about Dickens. You know about him? Of course—you've written on him.

Having asked about Ellen Ternan and agreed that Estella in *Great Expectations* reflected Dickens's feelings for her, he went on to say that Kate Perugini had sought his advice about publishing her father's letters to her mother. "I told her there was no reason they shouldn't be published; but privately I didn't think they showed much affection, except for brandy and turkey and sausages." He had, he said, loved Dickens ever since reading him as a boy, his favourites being *Little Dorrit* and *Great Expectations*. "But he was completely out of the movements of the times. I always annoy his admirers by saying that Dickens died of drink. It began in America when he took nothing but brandy during his lectures."

KINGSMILL: And opium.

89

SHAW: And opium? Ah, really. The truth is, he'd a very large and stupid family, and he had to earn all this money for them, and kept himself going with brandy and other poisons. He was really dead before *Edwin Drood*. Sapsea and Grewgious repeat all the old tricks, but the fire has gone out of them. That reminds me of a farce of mine. I had to secure the copyright of *Cashel Byron's Profession*, and wrote *The Admirable Bashville* for the purpose, and the Stage Society produced it. I wanted a burlesque actor, and at last I found the man. His name was Wyse. He seemed to have all the tricks at his finger-tips, but at the very first rehearsal I discovered that the lines which I had thought so funny weren't funny at all. (*He paused and looked incredulously at his visitors, who laughed incredulously.*) I asked Ben Webster what was the matter with Wyse, and he replied "Oh, he'll be all right on the night." But he was *not* all right on the night. All the tricks were there, but they weren't amusing. The audience laughed at the lines, because they could hear them, but not at the way they were said. The next day Wyse lay down on a sofa and died, and I realised that he'd been dead before the rehearsal. Well, the point of all this rigmarole is that people die before they're ready for burial, and Dickens was dead before *Edwin Drood*.

The talk flowed on, and Shaw mentioned Edmund Yates, to the satisfaction of Kingsmill, who, seeing his chance, opened his mouth.

PEARSON: What did you think of Edmund Yates?

SHAW: No one liked him. He was a bully. I had to write for him on fiction at five-pence a line, and I got very tired of it, and of having to sign myself F.B.—you know, Fred Bayham, a character in Thackeray's *Newcomes*. I aired my grievances, and received a letter from his secretary beginning "Mr. Yates requests me to inform you that . . ." Well, there's only one possible answer to an opening like that and I began my letter "I have yet to learn . . ." Things got better after that, and when Yates was dying I used to write to him to cheer him up. But I found out later that his family hadn't dared to read him my letters, for it seems he was frightened of me.

Shaw looked at his visitors; there was a brief pause, and he continued: "Isn't it strange that men like Newton and Bunyan should be so credulous—Bunyan so shrewd about life and so fantastic about the existence of Hell, and Newton, with all that mathematical genius of his, writing rubbish about the Biblical prophecies? Of course I know nothing about mathematics myself, and in my Charles II play I put in 'the perihelion of Mercury' to get a laugh. Did you like your father?" He fixed his eye on Kingsmill, who replied with enough realism, he hoped, to satisfy his host, and enough piety to satisfy himself.

"No one could be angry with Wells for long," said Shaw. "He frankly admits that his temper is hysterical. I remember meeting him the day after the appearance of an outrageous article which he had written on me. Really, I'd have been entitled to punch his head. But he was looking small and uneasy, and I just shook hands with him. Another time, when he was very angry with me, he wrote to me that everyone believed me to be homosexual and that he, Wells, had always denied it, but in future he wouldn't."

After nearly two hours, during which they had tea, the visitors rose and murmured in unison that it had been delightful to see him. "And why wouldn't it be?" said Shaw. Pearson told him not to come out, but although it was dark Shaw insisted, and accompanied them to the gate. He stood there drooping and motionless until the car began to move, when he waved them good-bye.

"I'm afraid I shall never be able to attack the dear old boy again with real gusto," said Kingsmill, and sighed.

A. E. W. MASON

Pearson, who in the course of his exhaustive investigations into the life and character of Conan Doyle, had spent a delightful day with A. E. W. Mason at Petworth, took Kingsmill round to his flat at 51 South Street after tea on November 7. They were to have visited him in September, but their visit had been postponed owing to an accident, Mason having broken a rib while sleep-walking during a very vivid dream, in which he was taking some information of vital importance to the Pétain trial—whether helpful or prejudicial to Pétain he could not remember when he awoke.

They were pleased on arriving to find their host had fully recovered, and was back at work again on a book that was placed in the time of the Roman Empire. Kingsmill having disclaimed much knowledge of that period, Mason handed him a pamphlet on the Roman Emperors—a concise and lucid summary of their careers. Skimming it, Kingsmill was relieved to find that the handful of Emperors who had escaped assassination had fallen on the field of battle, with a reasonable presumption that they had been picked off from the rear. "Our planet," he said, "seems to have survived all this quite comfortably, so why shouldn't it survive our late enemies and our present allies?"

"Stalin interests me very much," said Mason. "I wish we knew more about him. Those trials—what do the confessions *mean*? How are they obtained and how genuine are they? There's something very queer there. I've been told of a case in which a man—not a Russian—absolutely declines to speak if the subject is ever brought up. Queer!"

Kingsmill, mentioning that he had recently re-read Mason's mountaineering novel, *Running Water*, added that he had sometimes wondered how many purposive accidents had taken place in the Alps in Victorian days. "It might," he said, "be worth going through old files of *The Times* to trace the eminent professors, the Harley Street physicians, the judges, statesmen, bishops and bankers who returned from Switzerland in a distracted state owing to their wives having lost their footing crossing crevasses or on tracks winding above boiling torrents."

"And," interposed Pearson, "I presume, revolting and unnatural though the idea is, there may have been a few stricken widows, too."

"It hadn't occurred to me before," said Mason, "but that may be why *Running Water* sent so many people to Switzerland."

"I've just been enjoying your book on Drake," Pearson said, "and I hope you'll give us another man of action."

"I've always wanted to write on Blake," replied Mason, "but whenever I mention it people always think I mean the poet. There are some first-rate fragments—his defence of Taunton, his amazing courage at Bristol, and of course those wonderful naval actions, but there's not enough material for a full-length study.''

''Have you read Johnson on Blake?'' asked Pearson.

''Johnson? Did he write on him?''

''Yes.''

''Is it good?''

''Not very.''

''Ah!–One of the very few personal details recorded about him is that the Dean of Christ Church thought him too short and insignificant to be admitted as a Fellow.''

''Well, if you can't do Blake,'' said Pearson, ''what about that short but highly significant man Hanaud–Sherlock's only worthy successor; and Hanaud, unlike Sherlock, can fill out a long novel.''

He had just finished an Hanaud book, Mason said, and showed them a page proof, which they handled with expectant relish.

The talk turned to Dumas and ended on Balzac, whose honeymoon journey with Madame Hanska from Dresden to Paris was, Mason said, a most dramatic episode, concluding as it did with the madness and suicide of the servant empowered by Balzac to get his Paris mansion ready for the arrival of his aristocratic bride.

As they walked back to the Club, Pearson and Kingsmill sang Mason's praises in a duet which may not have been musical, but was at least heartfelt. Over dinner, Kingsmill remarked on a perceptible uneasiness in Shaw when he was dismissing Bunyan's belief in an afterlife as absurd. Perceiving a perceptible uneasiness in Pearson, whose failure to disbelieve in immortality Kingsmill believed to be a source of some discomfort, he continued pacifically ''There's a lot to be said for personal survival on this side of the grave, too. Our present time of life has much to recommend it.''

PEARSON: Yes, it's far pleasanter now than when we were younger. One has a great store of things to look back upon and real internal tranquillity. But how terribly fast life goes at our age! I realised the other day that it is already two years since Shaw's wife died. We'll be dead before you can say 'knife.'

KINGSMILL: Knife.

PEARSON: Fork.

KINGSMILL: Your trick.

HIBERNATION

As the winter was now coming on, and extended journeys were no longer practicable, Pearson and Kingsmill decided to start putting their notes into shape; but before opening their indoor cam-  paign they called on Marjory Whittington to find out what fruit her journeys had borne, and how far her view or views of London conformed with theirs. After tea with her in the Albany, much enlivened by her telling vignettes of the Albany and its residents during the air raids, she showed them some drawings of notable London buildings, and also some delightful little sketches of out-of-the-way scenes and places that had taken her fancy, and seemed much relieved when they begged her to follow her fancy wherever it took her, even if it took her round London. On this note they parted, engaging to meet her again in a few months to resurvey the situation.

DISTANT CONTROL

On Wednesday, November 14, Pearson and Kingsmill went to see the two parts of *Henry IV*, lunching previously at the Connaught Rooms. Before lunch, at the bar, Arnold Gibbons, a friend and colleague of Colin Hurry, unfolded to Kingsmill the story of his psychical relationship with Madame Du Barry, whose life he was writing. A dark, square-jawed, urbanely determined man, with a trenchantly dramatic narrative style, Gibbons fixed Kingsmill with his eye and began: "Shortly after the last war, I was organising –but it doesn't matter what I was organising. Suffice it that one afternoon I found myself in a large room in Carlton House Terrace. A party was in progress–a festive party, if I may so put it–and a lion, a china lion, broke loose and shot across the polished floor towards a glass cabinet. I, Sir, took in the situation at a glance, and, diving forward, caught the beast just as its nose penetrated the glass. On the shelf of that cabinet, Sir, was ranged a dinner service stamped with the arms of Madame Du Barry."

KINGSMILL: Good God!

GIBBONS: On another occasion, Sir, as I was walking along Euston Road, on the south side, I collided with a gentleman who was carrying a number of books. They dropped to the ground–thud! thud! thud! I made the necessary apologies, retrieved the books–thus! and we fell into talk. Taking me to his nearby quarters, he ushered me into his library. On a bracket, directly facing me, stood a bust of Madame Du Barry.

KINGSMILL: Good God!

GIBBONS: On a further occasion, Sir . . . Madame Du Barry.

KINGSMILL: Good God!

GIBBONS: You will not, I think, question, Sir, that something other than mere chance is at work here, and that I have not chosen my subject, but my subject has chosen me.

A brief and pregnant silence was broken by Kingsmill, who said rather tentatively "I'm afraid I don't know much about Madame Du Barry, but am I right in supposing that she showed some reluctance to . . . that when she was on the way to the guillotine, she more or less lost her nerve?"

Gibbons fixed Kingsmill with his eye–"Yes," he said, quietly. "She was unique in that."

HENRY IV

"For the first time in the history of the world," said Pearson, as they left the theatre after the curtain had fallen on Falstaff's disgrace, "human eyes have been privileged to witness the two parts of *Henry IV* on the same day. That is wonderful enough, but what is even more wonderful is that for the first time in my forty years of playgoing, I've seen an imaginative Falstaff. All the others were super-Bardolphs. They knew that they looked fat, and they thought that if they also hiccoughed, no one could in reason ask more.

KINGSMILL: Yes, Ralph Richardson was not merely a comic man who to his surprise eventually comes unstuck. What particularly impressed me was the note of foreboding when Falstaff says 'Banish plump Jack, and banish all the world!' This showed the fear that was always there beneath his humour, the knowledge that pleasure will be paid one time or another, and prepared one for his end, which moved me almost like Lear's.

PEARSON: Richardson must play Lear, and Olivier, who was very amusing as Shallow and very picturesque as Hotspur, must play Mark Antony—both Antonys, Caesar's friend and Cleopatra's lover. I hope Richardson and Olivier stick together. A notable pair!

NEW YEAR'S DAY

On New Year's Day, just before lunch, Kingsmill entered the bar of the Authors in a state of exhilaration. "Everyone I've passed in the street looks happy," he said. "I suppose because the most unpleasant year in our lifetime is over—Belsen, Bombs, peace with Germany followed almost immediately by peace with Japan, and life on our hands again, a prospect which only a convinced believer in personal immortality can stomach. Are you with me, Graham?" he exclaimed, smiting Graham Greene on the shoulder. 'Oh, I forgot, you're a Catholic."

Graham Greene looked disturbed. "Are you well?" he asked. "Has anything happened?"

"I suppose things will right themselves in a day or two," said Kingsmill, in a conciliatory voice. "But, anyhow, that's how matters stand to-day."

Graham, shaking his head, finished his drink and left the bar, sobered.

FIRST AID FROM MALCOLM MUGGERIDGE

On the following evening Pearson and Kingsmill dined with Malcolm Muggeridge at the Café Royal.

Malcolm had been reading Froude's *Carlyle* and, while not expressing any great sympathy for Carlyle, declined to agree with Kingsmill that Mrs. Carlyle was in any way or in any degree to be pitied. Jane, he said, wanted glory and deserved what she got; Thomas wanted mothering and got what he deserved.

Kingsmill having remarked that he had recently heard that there had, after all, been a woman in Macaulay's life, but the details were immured in some subterranean vault and could hardly come to the surface without the help of an atom bomb, Malcolm said that with a little thought it should be possible to reconstruct the affair without Stalin's assistance.

"She was clearly the widow of a Calcutta writer," he said, "and her husband had been a promising young fellow. Macaulay, during his time in India, noticed him and predicted that he would go far. But he went still farther, leaving a widow and, I think, a still-born child."

KINGSMILL: 'It was better so,' the Victorian formula for the passing of any member of a family except an uninsured breadwinner. But what makes you so certain that India was where Macaulay met his fate?

MUGGERIDGE: There's an excitement in his Warren Hastings essay which points to some personal memory—the description of Baroness Imhoff's cabin as fitted up by Warren, her lover. It's all connected, it's all connected.

PEARSON: But how did Macaulay's affair with the widow come to a head?

MUGGERIDGE: She called on him when they were both back in England, and he gave her a little help. The little became more, but Macaulay was too cautious to take the plunge, and things might have dribbled along like this indefinitely, if she hadn't invented a warrant-officer who was making honourable proposals to her. A fantastic notion, but it decided Macaulay . . .

KINGSMILL: After he'd dredged his amazing memory for examples from life and literature of widows who had received honourable proposals.

MUGGERIDGE: He set her up in a couple of rooms off Church Street, Kensington. His only confidant was that legal friend of his, T. Ellis, who was empowered in the event of Macaulay's death to continue the widow in the receipt of two-sevenths of her previous allowance.

PEARSON: But, damn it, Malcolm, Macaulay was a very generous man!

MUGGERIDGE: And wasn't that generous, Hesketh? Haven't you visualised her?

PEARSON: I'm beginning to.

Turning to Kingsmill, Malcolm said that he had been giving further and more careful thought to the question of what men in the past he would like to have been, and had decided on Chaucer, Johnson, Cromwell and St. Augustine.

PEARSON: On what principle have you arrived at this odd collection?

MUGGERIDGE: Well, Chaucer as poet, Johnson as a human being, Cromwell as a man of action, and Augustine as a saint.

KINGSMILL: Augustine's not my idea of a saint.

MUGGERIDGE: Don't forget we're discussing who we *want* to be, not who we *ought* to be. I hope to become a saint, but in due course, and Augustine wasn't in any hurry either.

KINGSMILL: I see. Who are your four, Hesketh?

PEARSON: On Malcolm's basis, one for each of the main types, I'd be Shakespeare for literature, Johnson for character, Fielding for action, and myself for saintliness.

KINGSMILL: All the main types being writers?

PEARSON: Exactly.

KINGSMILL: And, of course, waiving the matter of your saintliness, Fielding cleaning up the gangsters of London beats most things in the way of action.

MUGGERIDGE: And what's your choice, Hughie?

KINGSMILL: Disregarding your categories, I think my four would be Shakespeare, Beethoven, Wordsworth and Constable, with Johnson, Cervantes, Rembrandt and Mozart as a reserve team in case of need.

MUGGERIDGE: In case of what need?

KINGSMILL: But if I must conform with your ruling, I think I'd choose Wordsworth for poetry, because he was so much happier and more tranquil than Shakespeare that in my own interests I must prefer him. Then Johnson as a human being, of course, in spite of his melancholia. And Cromwell, I suppose, if one has to be a man of action. And François de Sales is my favourite saint.

MUGGERIDGE: A very wise selection, Hughie.

KINGSMILL: Oh, that's it, is it? I see what you mean, and agree that horse-faced Wordsworth, and Johnson with his convulsions, and Cromwell with his warts, and François dedicated to God at the age of twelve, would between them drive Messalina into the nearest convent. Very well, I substitute Shakespeare for Wordsworth—that balances or over-balances your Chaucer—and St. Paul for François de Sales. Thorn for thorn, I doubt if there's much to choose between your saint and mine.

Ranging over other people they would like to have been, they were unanimous in agreeing that they would not like to have been Coleridge. "Not," said Pearson, "that one actually dislikes him; but he's so amorphic, a sort of oyster on two legs, or a penguin flapping his useless wings, unable to fly, and boring everybody to death with the principles of flight."

KINGSMILL: But did Coleridge mind being Coleridge? We are rather tending to mix up what we think of these men with what they thought of themselves? It probably depressed him at times, but, being so shapeless, the pain wasn't sharp. On the other hand, Carlyle's vituperative raging at the universe and everyone and everything in it suggests acute and permanent self-dissatisfaction.

PEARSON: Nothing to the dissatisfaction Jane felt with him—poor Jane, cooped up with that diseased and screaming egotist.

MUGGERIDGE: You needn't pity Jane. It's obvious from the numerous references in Froude to her passionate addiction to the novels of Balzac and George Sand that Carlyle's inability to compete with even the feeblest Parisian who crawls across their pages was something she never allowed him to forget. It's equally clear that the poor wretch was always dipping into Sand and Balzac in the hope of picking up tips on how to deal with Jane. The climax came that time they were up in Scotland together. Froude tells it all rather badly, but it's clear enough that Tam, whom Jane had been flaying more ferociously than ever, couldn't stand it any longer and rushed off to some out-of-the-way spot where he could give his undivided attention to Balzac and Sand, Jane meanwhile going to a seaside cottage where she could read Sand and Balzac in peace. And then one afternoon, when she was pleasantly relaxed on her sofa, the door is flung open and Tam stumbles across the threshold with bloodshot eyes and clawing hands.

KINGSMILL: 'Whaur's your Honoré de Balzac noo?' I see. Well, Malcolm, you've brought a little colour into some gray lives, and I'm sure both Macaulay and Carlyle would thank you for it.

From literature they passed to politics, and the imminent meeting of U.N.O.

MUGGERIDGE: Why do politicians bother to finish their sentences? Everyone present knows exactly what's coming after the opening words. For instance, Attlee's speech at the first meeting of U.N.O. would be just

as intelligible and just as stirring if abbreviated as
follows:

On this historic occasion when . . .
There can be no one here present who . . .
We have just passed through an ordeal that . . .
No thinking man will underestimate the . . .
While there are many circumstances which . . .
There are solid grounds for hoping that . . .
The Nations of the World here gathered together
for . . .
It is surely incumbent on all of us to . . .
While recognising the reality of . . .
No mere conflict of interest should . . .
The immeasurable strides that Science has . . .
Such is the choice that at present confronts . . .
It is idle to think that the politicians can . . .
It rests with the common peoples to . . .
With head erect and clear purpose, we . . .
That goal towards which the Nations of the World
are . . .

A SIMPLE LUNCH

A lunch in Colin Hurry's honour given by a well-known
restaurateur, on January 21, included Pearson and Kingsmill among the guests. During the lunch their host told
Kingsmill that as most of Colin's friends were writers, he

had felt that they would prefer a simple lunch, not "a palate searcher."

In an ante-room there was a buffet loaded with plates of oysters (and kickshaws for those who did not care for oysters); also a dry white wine harmonising with oysters and kickshaws. The lunch itself opened with a Bortsch, and a sherry. Then came guinea-fowl with mushroom sauce, and a garniture of cunningly devised vegetables. Champagne (1941 vintage) accompanied this course. The sweet was an ice with white grapes and sliced peaches, and this was followed by a cheese savoury made of a matured cheese. The dessert was half a pound of hot-house grapes to each guest. A magnum of port, liqueur brandy, cigars and coffee rounded off the meal.

After lunch Pearson and Kingsmill approached James Mitchell, who was displaying the strange merriment of a post-prandial Scot, and informed him that they had reached him in their book. "We're warming up to you," said Kingsmill. "That's right, my boy," cried Mitchell. "Warm up, warm up! Don't pull your punches. I look forward to a ripe old age on the damages." He shook with wild and silent glee.

PLAGUE AND ANTIDOTE

Kingsmill, in an unstable condition even before this lunch, tried in vain to regain his balance during the rest of the month, and took to his bed at the beginning of February. One day, when his concern for himself had reached its peak, he was told, and could just grasp, that Mrs. Pearson had rung up to say that her husband was ill, and would he wait for news before coming along to work?

On Monday, February 11, Pearson and Kingsmill were sufficiently convalescent to meet at the Club. Pearson, shocked by the appearance of his friend, who had lost between two and three stone, said "Why call this wasting pestilence 'flu? It is the authentic plague of the Elizabethan Age, for which doctors can do as little now as they did then, but grasping, like everyone else to-day, at any jargon that takes the sting out of reality, they call it 'flu, a pretty caressing monosyllable. I wonder they don't call it the Magic 'Flu; that would make it an even pleasanter thing to die of."

KINGSMILL: It's heightened my sense of smell, I suppose because I can't smoke. No wonder people smoke or drink or dope. If one walks through a charnel-house, which is what the world appears to me at present, one doesn't want the olfactory powers desirable in the Garden of Hesperides, which I daresay is as disgusting as anywhere else. Pardon these harsh words, but the truth is that if Swift could have read my thoughts these last few days, he'd have passed respectfully by on the other side.

PEARSON: I don't know if I have had the plague as severely as you, but I agree with everything you say. My only escape, when the worst was over, was Stanley Weyman—*A Gentleman of France*.

KINGSMILL: And I've been reading his *Under the Red Robe*. Everything else got on my nerves, but he took me into a world where there was neither flesh, which I loathed in all its aspects, nor spirit, to which I wasn't equal, but a day-dream between the two.

Revived by a double whisky, Kingsmill continued "There's no one like him when life goes too far. I re-read *A Gentleman of France* two or three months ago, and pictured it coming to Weyman one spring morning in his middle thirties as he walked in Kensington Gardens, from time to time absently side-stepping a child's hoop, while old Paris formed round him, steep-roofed, with narrow, foul-smelling ways where the clash of steel on steel was too common a sight and sound to provoke more than a shrug of the shoulders in the passers-by. How would he have fared in such times? A ruffling gallant? Well, hardly that. But why not a sober gentleman, forty or so, of an ancient though impoverished family, with a strong sword wrist and a quick eye? At this point he would begin to warm up. Some wild slip of a girl would scorn him for his forty years and shabby attire. He'd be in charge of her on some dangerous journey, defend her again and again against almost hopeless odds, and be paid with bitter jibes, hiding her growing love. He would fall ill—the plague. She must not take it, and he would stagger away to die alone. But she would find him, her face would be bending over him as the fever left him. A couch of leaves in the green-wood, far from the stir and pain of life, a cool hand on his brow, love in her eyes at last. . . . And so, side-stepping another hoop, to lunch at the Savile."

PEARSON: Frankly, I shed buckets of tears over that greenwood scene the other day. But his daydream is all of a piece; nothing, not even the plague, jars one in it—fighting without bloodshed, high affairs without low affairs, riding without aches, landscapes without insects, and the final bliss untouched by fear, the ecstacy of love without its exactions.

THE FACE AT THE WINDOW

After ten days at the George, Battle, Kingsmill returned to town in tolerable repair. Having brought their book up to date, and in spite of spring coming before any sane swallow would have dared to, in the shape of snow-storms, sleet-storms, hail and frost, the two friends decided that they must sally forth in search of fresh material. Their preliminary reconnaissance, on March 8, took them as far as Bouverie Street. On their way back through Fountain Court, Pearson caught sight of Alan White, who was standing by his desk on the first floor of his office. A feeling of nostalgia came over the travellers as they saw, rather indistinctly, the publisher of *This Blessed Plot*. They remembered his delight in it, and recognised that it was not his fault, but Douglas Jerrold's misfortune, that he was not publishing their present book. Unlike Hamish Hamilton of *Skye High* fame, he had not made the great refusal. In spite of Pearson's protest, Kingsmill, picking up a stone, threw it at Alan's window, and a moment later Alan's enquiring face appeared behind the pane, which was still intact. On seeing them, he beckoned vigorously, and they went round to him by Essex Street. "When your stone hit the window I thought the electric light had fused," he said, as they seated themselves. "It's always doing that nowadays. Well, it's very nice to see you two again." Turning to Pearson, whose Life of Oscar Wilde he was shortly bringing out, he said "Oscar is subscribing very beautifully in the country."

"That's just the kind of charming thing he would do," said Pearson. "And you will find that he'll subscribe just as beautifully when he comes to town."

Having engaged to visit Alan in the country as soon as spring was safely over, the travellers went on their way.

THE ABBEY

In the forenoon of Thursday, March 14, Pearson and Kingsmill set out from Whitehall Court in bitter weather, arriving ten minutes later at their destination, Westminster Abbey. The northern entrance was closed, to the relief of Pearson, who said that it saved them from passing the politicians' statues in the north transept, a jungle of monumental masonry. Asked by Kingsmill how old the Abbey was, Pearson replied that it was mostly thirteenth century, but he had an idea the towers were later, and would verify the matter in due course.

In the western porch there was a notice—

LUNCH HOUR ADDRESSES
April 3. Prayer—What is it for?
April 10. Prayer—How is it done?

"Considering all the money spent on this building," said Kingsmill, "they might have settled these elementary points before now. However . . ."

They entered the Abbey, and as they were looking at the grave of the Unknown Warrior, an elderly woman came up and asked if they could direct her to the Civil Dead Memorial. Pearson suggested that she should consult the verger. She looked as if she had been crying, perhaps for her husband who had been killed in an air raid, and seemed in some degree soothed at the prospect of seeing the Memorial. Pearson, reading the inscription on the Unknown Warrior's grave, and casting a glance round, remarked "In view of the crowd of nonentities with which this place is cluttered up, I dispute the accuracy of 'They buried him among the Kings.' Let's search for some of these sovereigns."

They examined the southern wall of the side aisle, and discovered memorials to John Thomas, who died in 1793, Katherine Bovey, who was buried in Gloucester in 1724, Zacharia Pearce, who passed out in 1774, and Sir Palmer Fairborne, apparently of immortal memory, who was killed at Tangier in 1680. "But here," said Pearson, "*is* someone whom we, at any rate, know of: Major André, the subject of a poem by Anna Seward and the betrothed of her greatest friend, Honora Sneyd. Do you remember Anna's poem in which she indicted George Washington for murdering André, and how rapturously she withdrew the charge when a special envoy from the President came to Lichfield after the war to lay before her the true facts which, as they were arranged by Washington, naturally exonerated him from all guilt."

"Here at last," said Kingsmill, pausing before a bust of Clive, "is someone whom the Unknown Warrior would accept as a reasonable substitute for a king, but I see that they say nothing about his life, presumably because they don't want to refer to his death. Excusable, however. After all, suicide is not a lapidary theme. This gentleman underneath Clive, one William Wragg, appears from the space given him to have made a better end."

Pearson, who was reading the inscription with a gathering

frown, said "I see that he skinned out of South Carolina at the time of the American revolution, abandoning his wife and family. It says here that it was his loyalty to George III which compelled him to leave his distant family and ample fortune. If his fortune had been secure, he would undoubtedly have stopped with it, and therefore with his family. As it was, I imagine he took as much of it as he could with him, and I am glad to see he was shipwrecked, or more probably thrown overboard, off the coast of Holland in 1777."

THE POET'S CORNER

The first bust that attracted their attention as they turned into Poet's Corner was John Dryden's. "Swinburne," said Kingsmill, "applies Browning's lines about a brutal Roman Emperor with gross jaw and griped lips to Dryden. He does it in admiration, of course; but I am sure the notion of Dryden as a blustering gladiator is all wrong. Johnson tells us Dryden was bashful in company, and I get the same impression from this bust. He looks very sensitive, humane and even shy, rather like a more reserved and dignified and less histrionic Heine. And his verse corresponds with his appearance. . . ."

PEARSON: . . . Being both kindly and delicate. Because Pope is finnicky, Dryden is considered coarse. The real distinction is that Dryden is exactly right and that Pope is superfine. People talk about Dryden's bludgeon and Pope's rapier, but you can search all through Pope without finding anything as neat and concise as 'They got a villain and we lost a fool.' I needn't add that it's kindly, because it breathes benevolence in every syllable.

They passed by the busts of Tennyson and Longfellow, who were trying without success to look like themselves and unlike each other. Dwarfing a modest memorial stone to Chaucer was an impressive tablet to John Roberts, Esq.– The very faithful secretary of Henry Pelham, Minister of State to King George. Wondering which of these three was the poet, Roberts, Pelham or George, the travellers passed musing by, and raising their eyes beheld the disgusted countenance of Samuel Butler, whose expression suggested the state of mind in which he wrote:–

> "'Tis a strange age we've lived in, and a lewd,
>   As e'er the sun in all his travels viewed. . . .
>   Twice have we seen two dreadful judgments rage,'
>   Enough to fright the stubborn'st-hearted age. . . ."

"Poor old man!" murmured Pearson. "He lives through the age of Cromwell, passes through the dreadful judgments of Plague and Fire, and while the Restoration is laughing over his satire on the Puritans, he dies in poverty and neglect."

To their left was an almost illegible memorial stone to Michael Drayton, surmounted by a bust, the expression of which was petulant but showed signs of outworn charm. " 'A proper goodly page,' in his youth," murmured Kingsmill. "Rather like Rupert Brooke, I should think, but outlived his inspiration, it seems."

Circling round an enormous bust of Adam Lindsay Gordon, the famous Australian horseman, they came to a more than life-size statue of Thomas Campbell, looking

complacent if faintly apologetic, as though conscious that
he was overshadowing William Wordsworth, who was
cowering behind him in a dressing-gown. Close by was
Nollekens' bust of Johnson, on which Johnson had
remarked "I think my friend, Joe Nollekens, can chop out
a head with any of them."

Attracted by a large monument on the other side of
the transept, they glanced quickly at Coleridge, who was
looking upwards with an expression which deprecated
without rejecting whatever benefits Heaven might be
pleased to divert in his direction, at Robert Burns, represented as usual with a turnip face and a turn-up nose, and at
Sir Walter Scott, who seemed to be watching the public to
estimate what it would require in the book line during
1946. The large monument was, they learned, to Sir
Thomas Robinson and wife, and it appeared that Sir
Thomas had been diverted from poetry to the Governorship
of Barbados, where he had perhaps put his imagination at
the service of his accounts, for the inscription stated that
"On some complaints he was recalled, though in justice
to his memory it must not be concealed that the complaints
were afterwards substantially acknowledged to be ground-
less."

Leaving the Poets' Corner, they crossed the main aisle
and examined a bronze candelabrum which, a verger
informed them, had been carved by a German refugee,
whom an English peer had financed. It was a massive piece
of work, representing figures from the Old and New
Testaments, and the travellers were pleased to find that
foreign art could look to the English nobility for support.

In front of the candelabrum were the graves of several
eminent scientists, and close by a small stone inscribed

J. Woodward, M.D. 1728. Pearson asking who he might be, the verger replied "There are lots of them about." He may, suggested Kingsmill, have cured the Dean of croup, but here the verger could not help them. The cold outside was intense, and they returned by taxi to the Club.

WESTMINSTER CATHEDRAL

After lunch they took a Victoria bus, on their way passing the Cathedral of Methodism, which they noticed was called Central Hall in one place and Midland Bank in another, evidence, they hoped, that God and Mammon had at last come to an understanding.

Dismounting in Victoria Street they proceeded towards Westminster Cathedral. "The later marzipan period," observed Pearson, glancing up at it. They took the lift to the top of the tower; and, perhaps partly influenced by the east wind, found the view depressing, such greenery or water as they saw seeming to them to be in the wrong place and not enough of it, lost, as it were, in a dull morass of indistinguishable buildings. Descending, they examined the interior of the Cathedral. The dull red brick was in process of being covered by marble tiling, with a garish effect which, in the opinion of the travellers, did not augur well for the future. They hoped, however, that at least the sombre and impressive dome might be spared. "The Norman–Gothic style," said Pearson, "is what suits the English climate and character. These marble effects may be all very well in dark Italian interiors, cunningly contrived to exclude a blazing sun. Here, in England, we have the sun in better control, and can allow it to flood through our wonderful Gothic windows and bathe our grey stone in a gentle radiance." "It's all Luther's fault," said Kingsmill. "If he hadn't thought of Protestantism, the Catholics wouldn't have thought of Catholicism. England is naturally Anglican, and ought to contain nothing but Norman and Gothic churches. Nowadays, thanks to Luther, we have on the one hand the Midland Bank and on the other this incipient Turkish Bath."

After tea at the Authors, the travellers were joined by Patrick Dobbs and Douglas Jerrold, who, though a Catholic, replied, in answer to a leading question, "I must admit that the Abbey is the better building, on the whole." Then, passing over to the offensive, he asked them if they had seen Marjory Whittington.

"Yes," said Pearson.

"And do her drawings conform with the text?"

"No," said Pearson.

PATRICK DOBBS (*suddenly*): Are you going to describe the Alexandra Palace?

PEARSON: Whatever we see, we describe.

JERROLD: Apparently not a very exacting programme.

KINGSMILL: Our book may not be of much use to Stalin if he wants something for street-to-street fighting, but it will preserve the essence and spirit of London for our Patagonian readers a thousand years hence.

At last the winter relented, and Wednesday, March 20, was a mild spring day. The friends had decided to visit Eton and Windsor, and Kingsmill, as they set off from the Club, said how extraordinary it was that he should have reached his later fifties without ever having set eyes on either of them. They travelled by the 12.20 for Slough in a third-class carriage, as the Great Western Railway had seemingly found it useless to provide first-class accommodation for visitors to Windsor and Eton.

On the way they outlined a Doctor Johnson film.

PEARSON: There certainly wasn't a film in Johnson before you established the importance of Mrs. Thrale in his life; but now, with a judicious use of the triangle drama, Piozzi–Mrs. Thrale–Johnson, it would be a winner. The great old solitary breaking his heart while the romantic Italian musician brings love at last to the exquisite woman whose emotions her dull brewer husband had never touched.

KINGSMILL: Who would you cast for the Great Old Solitary?

PEARSON: Ralph Richardson, of course.

KINGSMILL: And Greer Garson for Mrs. Thrale. Anyone less like that mother of twelve children, who even as a young girl would have left me at least completely calm, I cannot imagine. Incidentally, it would be blasphemy to saddle Greer Garson with more than two of Thrale's children at the outside.

PEARSON: Two it shall be. Now for Piozzi–Charles Boyer, of course; and what about Charles Laughton for Mr. Thrale? He's subtle enough to show suspicion of

Piozzi contending in the brewer's stagnant mind with the dreadful fear that death, which he felt approaching, might claim him before the first lampreys of the season reached his table.

KINGSMILL: With a love drama in full spate, the public could stomach a little of Johnson in his more familiar aspects, couldn't it?

PEARSON: Yes; and after seeing him as Mr. Puff, I don't hesitate to cast Laurence Olivier for Boswell. And as we, in a well-ordered world like this, will naturally be producing the film, it will be very pleasant for us to repeat our 1937 tour to the Hebrides. Richardson and Olivier will precede us on foot, and on Shetland ponies for the passage of Mam Rattigan, and we shall follow in a car.

KINGSMILL: It would be a pity not to include Bonnie Prince Charlie. After all, he was in those parts only thirty years before Johnson. Having seen Edward G. Robinson as Lord Arthur Savile, I am prepared to see him as Bonnie Prince Charlie; and Merle Oberon as Flora MacDonald would help me to forget Merle Oberon as George Sand. They would only come in incidentally; and in order to keep the main theme well before the public, why shouldn't Piozzi's first meeting with Greer Garson be when he dives from the battlements of Dunvegan Castle to drag her from a watery grave?

As they alighted at Windsor, Kingsmill said how extra-ordinary it was that he should have reached his later fifties without ever having set eyes on the place. "Good, that settles the lunch problem," exclaimed Pearson, as he sighted the White Hart Hotel. "And how handily placed!" As they entered, they seemed transported back to their youth—ample, unobtrusive comfort, a liberal use of space, leisurely attentiveness, everything right and nothing planned. After lunch they visited St. George's Chapel. Pearson, speechless for a time at the beauty of the nave, became articulate on the subject of the choir screen—"It's the wickedest thing. They've ruined all our cathedrals by putting up those unsightly objects. The Englishman's hatred of beauty."

Wandering round the Chapel, they looked at the tombs and memorials, which seemed to be more or less confined to members of the Royal Family, and so were surprised to come across a tablet dedicated to Alamaya, son of Theodore, King of Abyssinia, born 1861, died 1879. Underneath were the words "This tablet is placed here to his memory by Queen Victoria. 'I was a stranger and ye took me in.'"

"If that is the Theodore I am thinking of," said Pearson, "I should like to know how it came about that Queen Victoria took this stranger in. It may have been a very noble act on her part, but in order to guard against being taken in myself I shall consult an Encyclopaedia when we get back."

Approaching the choir screen, they peered through it and saw a small group listening to the explanations of a verger, who on sighting the travellers produced a key, and before they quite realised what was happening added them to his bag. After they had assimilated some interesting information about the Knights of the Garter whose arms adorned the stalls of the choir, Kingsmill reminded Pearson that they would be late for Mr. Jacobs, and the verger, producing his key, gave them back their freedom.

From the Castle terrace they looked down on the curving Thames, and the tall trees bordering the playing-fields of Eton and the turrets of the Chapel beyond and a rolling expanse of meadow-land stretching to a dim outline at which Pearson, pointing, said "A Distant Prospect of Harrow School."

"How wonderful this all is!" Kingsmill exclaimed. "People ought to know about it. Funny to think of this all here when I used to look in this direction from the churchyard at Harrow, vaguely aware of Windsor somewhere in the plains beneath."

ETON

Descending the hill, they crossed the Thames and found, what nothing they had read on the subject had prepared them for, that Eton was a town with a long high street of variegated and beautiful buildings leading to the school. They passed a house which Christopher Wren had built for himself in 1776; they passed a china shop, called the Cockpit, which dated from the fifteenth century; they passed a number of Georgian houses still, for all they knew to the contrary, inhabited by Jane Austen characters, and came at last to the College itself. Passing through the beautiful quadrangle, which Pearson thought as fine as anything in Cambridge and Kingsmill finer than anything in Oxford, they entered the Chapel, where Pearson read the last chapter of the Epistle to the Galatians from the superb New Testament on the lectern. "The greatest piece of prose in all literature," he murmured as he came to the end. Kingsmill wondered if it would be a feasible project to remove the two magnificent volumes from the lectern. "As we haven't brought a carpet bag," he said, "you'll have to take the New Testament, as you seem to prefer it, and I'll take the Old. If anyone stops us, we are under instructions from the Head Master, who wishes to have them rebound in his favourite colour. How far would we get, do you think?"

"Home; but we'd have to put them back before the police identified us with the two individuals who, according to the hall-porter at the White Hart, had left these suspicious-looking volumes with him while they were at tea."

On emerging from the College they crossed a road and went down a street bordered by buildings which they supposed were the school houses. A squad of boys in khaki was being dismissed, and after this painful incident was closed, Kingsmill approached a woman who was wheeling a baby, and asked her if these were indeed school houses. Her information coming to him rather indistinctly through the baby's roars, he thanked her at the top of his voice, and rejoined Pearson. Proceeding on their way, they stopped a boy of about seventeen, who with the courtesy of one who does not wish to overpraise what is his, and the conviction of one who has assessed it at its true value, urbanely replied "Yes, all these rather barrack-like buildings are school houses," and turned into one of them.

The street soon petered out into low meadow-lands, beyond which they saw the railway viaduct and along it a train hurrying towards Slough, its wheels, as usual on these branch lines, revolving very quickly, as though the engine were conscious of its antiquity but resolved to show that the old man was as good as any of these streamline youngsters.

As they walked back to catch a bus into Windsor, Kingsmill remembered that he was in some danger of forgetting that beautiful buildings and august traditions do not necessarily elevate and inspire those within the range of their influence. "In case," he said, turning to his friend, "you are in the fortunate position of not knowing the Eton Boating Song, which is virtually the school anthem, the actual one being in Latin, here is a verse from it—

> Twenty years hence this weather
> Will tempt us from office stools.
> We may be slow on the feather
> And seem to the boys old fools,
> But we'll swing, swing together,
> And swear by the best of schools.

PEARSON: Good God!

KINGSMILL: I don't want to say anything harsh, especially as this visit is proving so delightful, but if that verse had been composed by one of the larger apes, it would have been hailed by the orthodox as conclusive proof of an impassable gulf between man and the animal creation.

Getting into the bus, the conductress of which was a little surprised when Kingsmill asked her if she did not think

Eton a wonderful place, they returned to Windsor, and once more enjoyed the Victorian comfort and peace of the White Hart.

VICTORIAN PEAKS

After dinner at the Club, Pearson looked in the Encyclopaedia for details of Theodore and his son Alamaya. "It appears," he remarked, "that the stranger whom Queen Victoria took in was indeed in parlous case. A British Expeditionary Force had penetrated into his father's dominions, flattened his father's capital, driven his father to suicide, and abducted his mother, who died during the forced march back to the coast. Alamaya himself, escaping his parents' fate, was brought to England, but on arriving there was sent to Rugby, and perished almost at once. In short, that memorial tablet is one of the peaks of Victorian insensitiveness, humbug and villainy."

"What are the other peaks?" asked Kingsmill, and Pearson, after a moment's reflection, replied: "Everest is undoubtedly Tennyson's King Arthur assuring his wife that he and God forgive her."

KINGSMILL: For Aconcagua I suggest Froude's view that when Mill staggered in on Mr. and Mrs. Carlyle, ghastly white and unable for some time to articulate a word, they were greatly relieved on learning that his state was due not to his having decided to elope with Mrs. Taylor, but merely to a housemaid having burnt the only MS. of Carlyle's French Revolution.

PEARSON: Popocatapetl is Thackeray leaving it an open question whether Becky Sharp was or was not innocent in her relations with the Marquis of Steyne—innocence in this case meaning that she'd looted the Marquis of some thousands of pounds in hard cash and jewellery whilst successfully dodging his attempts to get her into bed.

KINGSMILL: For Elburz I suggest Browning's *A Light Woman*, in which he pictures himself as a sort of altruistic Rasputin who, to save a youthful friend from ruin, steps forward and instantly focuses on his mature and illustrious person the amorous yearning of the woman courteously referred to in the title of the poem. "And round she turned for my noble sake" is the way he puts it, with an irony which, as the rest of the poem abundantly shows, is not meant to be taken seriously. At the same time he is careful to make it clear that his well-known fidelity to his wife's memory remained unimpaired. Having likened the woman to a ripe pear, ready to drop at a touch from his finger, he adds that he has "no mind to eat it, that's the worst!"; and the poem ends with his blaming himself, unimpeachable though his motives were, for blasting a woman's happiness by kindling desires which he had no inclination to gratify.

PLANNED COURTSHIP

PEARSON: I don't know much about Browning, but from the kind of impression I get of him in Victorian memoirs, I wouldn't have put my shirt, to say nothing of his, on his fidelity to Mrs. Browning even when she was alive. Whenever he enters a Victorian drawing-room, I always have a feeling that it was a near thing for the housemaid on the stairs.

KINGSMILL: And yet for the Victorians themselves he was the great model of love without lust, and as they had a unique faculty for seeing empty space when a haystack was planked down in front of them, Browning could pour out verse which would have drawn protests from Boccaccio without their apparently noticing that he wasn't writing like Mrs. Hemans. Here are some lines of his for which Swinburne, if he had written them, would have been hounded out of the country. It's the grand crescendo of a poem called *Too Late*, and what would have happened if Robert Browning had been in time you are about to hear.

> My queen shall have high observance, planned
> Courtship made perfect, no least line
> Crossed without warrant. There you stand,
> Warm, too, and white, too! would this wine
> Had washed all over that body of yours,
> Ere I drank it, and you down with it, thus!

What's the picture that conjures up for you?

PEARSON: A perfectly clear one. He is visualising himself with a girl in a tiled room. He has just sluiced a bucket or two of inexpensive but sufficiently palatable wine over her (Emu brand—out of bond), and as it pours off her, he seizes her in his arms and laps it up.

KINGSMILL: I'm afraid you're right; but a counsel for the defence could interpret it more favourably. He would argue that a female bath attendant is implied. She pours the wine over the girl, it is taken up, bottled, and (by this stage virtually a vintage wine) served to Robert Browning at lunch and dinner for some days—with the chill taken off, perhaps. Thus the proprieties are observed, and what Browning's thoughts may be as he drinks it are between himself and his Maker, and therefore no concern of the jury.

PEARSON: Well, your quotation is at least arresting, and to that extent raises my opinion of Robert Browning, whose verse I have never cared for at all.

KINGSMILL: I used to love him round about twenty. He wasn't so obviously sentimental as Tennyson, and the robust way in which he threw a haze round sex made my own haziness seem robust. And even now there are lines, though no complete poem, which move me as much as ever—

> Infinite passion, and the pain
> Of finite hearts that yearn

and

> I would we were boys as of old
> In the field, by the fold.

ARBUCKLE AVENUE

As they were discussing Browning, Graham Greene came over and joined them. He had recently been reading a life of James Thomson, and said a visit to a Vauxhall Bridge lodging-house where Thomson had once lived might be worth making. Kingsmill took down the number, 240, and promised that they would, in pursuance of their general scheme, examine this building for what light it might throw on the darkness of the poet who wrote

The City of Dreadful Night. On Kingsmill surmising that perhaps 240 Vauxhall Bridge Road might have been blitzed without much loss, Graham sighed and said that, for his part, what had hurt him most was the partial disappearance of Arbuckle Avenue—"You know the houses I mean, Hugh; that row of hotels facing the west side of Paddington Station." "I've seen the houses you mention," said Kingsmill, "and I remember Fatty Arbuckle on the screen, and why he was compelled to leave it. But that is all. However, I'm sorry for your loss, even if I can't measure it."

WINCHESTER

As they took their seats in the train for Winchester on Wednesday, March 27, Pearson said "How extraordinary it is that I, who have never missed an opportunity of seeing a cathedral and know every cathedral in England backwards, should be visiting Winchester Cathedral for the first time to-day." On the way down they talked without cessation until Kingsmill, suddenly feeling that he must conserve his energy, rolled up his overcoat, put it beneath his head and closed his eyes. "Well, here we are," said Pearson, and Kingsmill reversed the processes through which he had just been.

Emerging from the station, Kingsmill said that they ought to pool their knowledge of the place, which, he added, was, so far as he could judge at the moment, less beautiful than he had expected. "One thing I am certain about in connection with it," he said, "and that is that Frank Harris came here."

"You mean, that is one of the very few things you are certain about in connection with Frank Harris? But whence your certainty?"

"Because his reference, in one of his stories, to the quaint customs of the school is curiously incidental. It doesn't subserve any of his usual purposes. It throws no light on him as a Christian, a literary genius, a great lover, a revolutionary, or a financier. So I assume that some Wykehamist, running counter to the first principles of his foundation, did actually pass Frankie into those hitherto unviolated precincts."

PEARSON: I'll bet Alfred Douglas wasn't Frankie's cicerone.

KINGSMILL: Hal Fisher, on the other hand, would have believed Douglas capable even of that. At least he'd have believed it in 1908, when Douglas was still under a very thick cloud. I remember a walk which Fisher very stoically took with me, in his capacity as my tutor at New College, and how when, to enliven a saddening conversation, I asked him what he thought of Douglas, he replied curtly "The most disreputable of living Wykehamists."

PEARSON: All this isn't helping either us or Winchester, which has other associations. Jane Austen and Izaak Walton are buried in the Cathedral, Sydney Smith was at school here, Keats wrote his sonnet on Autumn near by, King Arthur is associated with the city, and King Alfred made it the capital of England.

KINGSMILL: That's cleared the air.

They came to the High Street, and Kingsmill expressed

his regret that he had judged the town by the environment of the station, adding that after their experience at Aberdeen he ought to have known better. "That hill with firs on it makes a wonderful background to this street. How tremendously a vista like that helps a town! Look at Dublin.

PEARSON: Look at Mexico City.

At the bottom of the street stood a statue of a huge warrior armed to the teeth and holding up his sword like a crucifix. Pearson said he must be Alfred, Kingsmill said he must be Arthur, and Late Victorian pedantry saved Kingsmill by a narrow margin, for it was Ælfred. Postponing their search for a statue to Arturus, the Brito-Roman chieftain, they retraced their steps up the beautiful old street, passing a shop, Allnut and Clemens, names which they surmised concealed Beau Brummell and Mark Twain. A passer-by told them that they would get a good lunch at the Royal Hotel, and turning into a narrow side street they had reached the hotel, which Kingsmill was preparing to enter, when Pearson exclaimed at the sight of an old house, and hurrying on, Kingsmill in his wake, came to rest opposite it. "That," said Pearson, "is the most beautiful William and Mary house I've ever seen, due no doubt to its being inset, which throws the wings forward in that fascinating way. Perfect!"

They lunched by a window overlooking a garden which still had the grace and formality of the eighteenth century, and there after lunch, Pearson's William and Mary house visible beyond the old brick wall, they smoked their pipes in the warm spring air.

"You are now," said Pearson, as they reached the Cathedral close, "about to see the largest nave in England. There are (I am passing on the knowledge of a lifetime) two main styles in the building, Norman and Gothic, how distributed I haven't the faintest idea. Well, there it is!" They paused to take in the length of the stupendous edifice. "It's overpowering," muttered Pearson. "It's like a great stone brontosaurus," said Kingsmill, "and certainly not what I had expected to find in the haunt of ancient peace which I have always understood Winchester to be."

The interior, with its surging roof and graceful Gothic windows, was less intimidating but no less magnificent than the exterior. Wandering through it, they reached the south transept. "Norman, this," said Pearson. "It's like a great fortress, guarding the nave and choir on this side."

They asked a verger where Izaak Walton was buried, and he took them in to what must once have been a side chapel off the south transept. Just as Kingsmill was beginning to wonder whether they would have to remember their appointment with Mr. Jacobs, the verger vanished, and they were at leisure to examine Walton's grave and the memorial window.

PEARSON: My only complaint against Walton is that he lived at a time when he could have collected the most valuable material about Shakespeare, instead of which he paid pious but not very illuminating tributes to those four worthies in that window, carefully omitting whatever clashed with his idea of worthiness, and that was a good deal in the case of Donne, if doubtless less in the cases of

George Herbert, Henry Wootton, and the venerable Hooker.

KINGSMILL: Walton looks very peaceful up there, fishing by that stream with the pleasant hill beyond. I remember Hugh Thomson's illustrations to him in the *Cranford* series, and his name always brings back Hugh Thomson's daydream England, the old coaching times seen from the steam age—people and houses just far enough away, diminished but distinct, a little Eden of jollity and careless content, far more appealing in certain moods than any heaven one must work to get into.

PEARSON: The homely fields and the comfortable cows and the well-nourished horses and the jovial huntsmen and the jocund host and the trim serving-maid smiling from the gallery of the hospitable inn—there are moments when I'd barter Shakespeare and Beethoven and all of them to become a native of that snug and happy land.

Behind the high altar they came upon two shrines, the first containing the remains of Henry, Cardinal Beaufort, who interested Pearson as a character in *Henry VI, Part II.* but was clearly, from the immensely elaborate appearance of his shrine, a character in his own right; the second containing his successor as Bishop of Winchester, William Waynflete, the founder of Magdalen College, Oxford.

The travellers pondered for a while on the stupendous wealth and power centred in this ancient see, but feeling that it was too late, so far as they themselves were concerned, to do anything about it, continued on their way, and were presently reconciled to their modest Christian lot by the gruesome spectacle of Stephen Gardiner's recumbent statue. Between the decapitated head of this prelate and his appallingly emaciated body there was a gap of some inches.

A quiet *Who's Who* statement of the facts of his career gave no clue to why he looked like a case which would have excited comment in Belsen; and the travellers could only surmise that there had been an original effigy to Gardiner which had been replaced by the Puritans with this present horror, in order to show their opinion of Queen Mary's chief agent in the burning of the Protestant martyrs. But why was it still there? Had no one noticed it since the Commonwealth? Or had it become a sort of mascot, a reminder to Heaven that, after all, suffering had a place of its own in the Anglican scheme. Charity, too, had a place, they realised, as they paused before a memorial to the Rev. Frederic Iremonger, Prebendary of Winchester, who died in 1820. His charity, they read, was "unbounded but judicious."

The tributes to Jane Austen on her tablet and on her tomb seemed to the travellers to emphasise her piety at the expense of her intelligence. Perceiving that his friend was biting his thumb, and appeared to be generating a good deal of unnecessary heat, Kingsmill said that, after all, this kind of thing was very restful, and would probably jar on Sir Stafford Cripps, should he inadvertently look in at the Cathedral while revisiting his and Sir Oswald Mosley's old school.

THE COLLEGE

Pearson's contracted brows relaxing, they made for the main entrance, where they asked two passers-by the way to the College. Both were strangers in those parts, and the third person they stopped, an ancient native, replied to Kingsmill's "Is the College near here?" with "That's the Cathedral." "Yes, I noticed it," said Kingsmill, glancing irritably at the colossal mass of masonry forty to fifty yards away. "However, thank you." Shrill cries issuing from a courtyard, Kingsmill murmured "These yipping nippers should prove useful"; and entering saw a placard bearing the words The Pilgrim's School, and a crowd of pilgrims between the ages of eight and twelve, who were throwing a ball about. Addressing a lively-looking small boy, Kingsmill opened with "I suppose this is the preparatory school for Winchester." "More or less," piped the infant, and proceeded to furnish Kingsmill with precise instructions which he had entirely forgotten by the time he rejoined Pearson, who had held himself aloof from this commerce with embryonic man.

Passing under two archways they found themselves in a red-brick quadrangle, beyond which a squad of boys in khaki were drilling, a spectacle which for a moment disturbed their delight in the hills that formed the background to the school playing-fields. Three boys in running-shorts, approached by Kingsmill, halted with the usual courtesy of schoolboys nowadays, and one of them described the nearby buildings. The exterior of the chapel did not tempt the travellers into exploring its interior, but they went into the Old School, a seventeenth-century hall still used for Speech Day and similar proceedings. Driven out at once by the intense cold within, Kingsmill waited impatiently for his friend, who issued some minutes later with a polar air which Kingsmill found rather provoking. However, they continued amicably on their way, passing through the grey stone quadrangle of the College, where a dozen or so of boys in gowns were sitting or standing against a sunny wall, reading or talking, but seeming to the two friends curiously unrelated to one another and to their surroundings, as though either they or the travellers were in a dream.

As they returned through the Close they agreed that the school did not stand up to the Cathedral as Eton stood up to Windsor. "Speaking as a Wykehamist," said Kingsmill, "this visit to William of Wykeham's other foundation confirms me in my feeling that, whatever his general merits, William would have done well to leave education alone."

ABOVE THE CITY

Searching for an uncrowded teashop, they entered and left one which was completely full, and climbed to the third floor of another, where their momentary relief at finding a spare table quickly evaporated as Pearson realised that he was hemmed in by babies and their attendant mothers. "Comfortable?" asked Kingsmill, and Pearson emitting a "no" through compressed lips, Kingsmill rose and led his friend downstairs and out into the open air, where, blinking once or twice, Pearson said "It's not that I loathe the little scum, but that I love peace, and there's no peace where there are either kids or dogs."

After tea at the Royal Hotel they descended the High Street, leaving Ælfred on their right, and, pausing on a bridge, looked down at the water swirling and foaming from a hidden mill. "That old building under which the water's pouring," said Pearson, "is in pleasant contrast with these narrow side streets with low, red-brick houses, which would be appropriate in Leicester or Northampton but are not what I expected to find in this haunt of ancient peace." Climbing the East Hill, Pearson with a comparatively springy step, Kingsmill leadenly, they seated themselves on a wooden bench, from which they had a wide view of the city with its vast Cathedral and castellated Bishop's Palace and the high downs all round.

PEARSON: There's something rather melancholy about this scene. Compare those downs with our downs—they're darker, somehow, and there isn't the same feeling of airy space as in Sussex.

KINGSMILL: A haunt of ancient war. One pictures Arturus lurking behind the bushes on that slope with his Round Table assassins.

PEARSON: And Ælfred luring the Danes into that tricky little gully.

KINGSMILL: And the long line of villainous Bishops down there, squeezing the poor villeins out of their last groat.

PEARSON: It all makes one rather glad to see that little railway with its gleaming track escaping into a wider and freer world.

They returned to the comfort of the Royal Hotel, and in the darkness after dinner strolled in the garden listening to the church bells.

PEARSON: One of the reasons why they move me so much is that their sound is unchanging from age to age, and Chaucer and Lady Jane Grey and Shakespeare and dear old Anna Seward all heard those chimes just as we hear them, and they accompany one's own journey in the same unchanging way. One's tastes take different forms from year to year, but church bells are always the same.

KINGSMILL: And so they both recall the transitory expectations of the past and, being unchanging themselves, promise something that does not pass away.

SLOW TORTURE

In the train to London the travellers sat opposite a major and his wife, both quite young. Each was reading a paper-covered book, the man with a look of settled vindictiveness, the woman as though she were performing a task which had long since numbed her capacity to suffer. Her book, the travellers managed to discern, was *The Diary of a Nobody*. What the man was reading they could not see. On reaching the end of his book the man steadied himself by focusing his eyes on an advertisement on the back page, and then lit a cigarette, from which he occasionally desisted to stare hopelessly at the window. The woman, having finished her book, pushed it between her cushion and the next one and closed her eyes without any change in the blankness of her expression.

The travellers had not entirely shaken off the contagion of this couple's gloom when, on reaching the tube platform at Waterloo, they were whirled to the opposite extreme by a man suddenly darting from one of the side passages and executing a rapid and complicated pirouette, pausing when he saw he was observed, and as soon as the travellers looked away completing his dance with intensified vigour, after which he moved down the platform with an air of hauteur. "No wonder," remarked Pearson, "that when I pointed Hanwell out to you on our way to Windsor you said 'Why these invidious distinctions?' "

KENNETH HARE

Pearson, who had been reading Kenneth Hare's *New Poems* and had not seen him for some years, asked him to dinner at the Club on April 2, and suggested to Kingsmill that he and Brian should join them.

Before the arrival of the visitors, Pearson said to Kingsmill that he had on several occasions recited Kenneth's "Immortality" in public, and that it had always been tumultuously received, and why was it not in *New Poems*?

KINGSMILL: It was an impromptu which came to Kenneth after he had published *New Poems*. He was lunching with my brother Arnold, who explained Pascal's Wager to him. You know what it is?

PEARSON: No, I don't.

KINGSMILL: It's Pascal's way of recommending Christianity to infidels. His argument is that if you believe in it you will be rewarded hereafter, if there is a hereafter, and if there isn't, it won't matter. Arnold must have driven his argument home with some vigour because Kenneth, as soon as he left him, was inspired to the verses which you mention and which you may now appreciate even more fully:

> This Immortality's the horse
> I'll put my shirt on, please.
> Some think his chest is weak, of course,
> And some don't like his knees.
>
> But there's pots to gain, as you're aware,
> If he wins, accordin' to plan,
> And there's naught to lose, for we shan't be there,
> If he proves an Also Ran.

PEARSON: What scope the lad has! It's remarkable that a fellow who can write such a witty thing as that is also capable of something which Keats could have been proud of—

> With joy and love they wore the golden day,
> And in his West they saw the great sun down,
> They saw the moon arise, the colour of hay,
> And all that sun-drenched land grow dull and brown.
> And now one star floats out above the town,
> A purple mist drifts low upon the leas,
> And spectral cattle dream beneath the trees.

Kenneth and Brian arriving, they sat down to dinner. Brian remained somewhat quiescent during the evening, only rousing himself at the name of Oliver Cromwell, whom Kenneth was damning for his barbarity at Drogheda, with many details fresh to his listeners of the cruelties he perpetrated there. Leaning forward and speaking with a measured calm which hardly concealed a cold ferocity, Brian said "That is completely new to me. I don't deny it. I don't accept it. I merely say that it is COMPLETELY . . . NEW . . . TO . . . ME." As he spoke he rose slightly, and on the last word bounced back into his old position.

This thunderclap having died away, Brian became reminiscent about an occasion when he was staying in a friend's house. The telephone in his bedroom rang early one morning, and he hurried to it in his pyjama jacket, having just divested himself of the nether part. The story closing here, and Kingsmill having demurred to it as a story, Brian agreed that certainly it was lacking in point.

Pearson turned to Kenneth and remarked on the wonderful way in which his poetry captured the spirit of Flanders. Kingsmill prophesying that Bruges would have a statue to Kenneth one of these days, Kenneth said that there had actually been a proposal to call a street Rue Kenneth Hare. Kingsmill said it would be a mistake for a writer to allow a street to be named after him until he was safely dead, adding that, painful though he had found it during his stay in Thonon to be dunned by the local tradesmen, it would have been far more painful had their bills been sent from the Rue Hugh Kingsmill.

YE OLDE

Kenneth, asked by Pearson what he thought of Hugh Thomson's drawings, remembered them with difficulty. They were rather Ye Olde, weren't they? he asked.

KINGSMILL: And why shouldn't they be? There's a lot of nonsense talked along those lines by people who pretend they can bear only genuine antiques. A genuine antique is one thing; a piece of furniture or a drawing or a poem which expresses a nostalgia for the past is another. Shakespeare's *As You Like It* is Ye Olde, his sonnet on ladies dead and lovely knights is Ye Olde . . .

PEARSON: Keats is often Ye Olde, Tennyson is often Ye Olde. Ditto Scott. Ditto Balzac. Every age which is sufficiently civilised not to be exclusively interested in itself produces idealised pictures of the past. In his last quartets Beethoven himself created a perfect little dance in a pattern which would have delighted Purcell, and if Ye Olde is good enough for Beethoven, it's good enough for me.

Kenneth, with old-world courtliness, concurred.

JOE MAIDEN

On Wednesday, April 3, the two friends lunched at the Connaught Rooms with James Mitchell and Joe Maiden.

KINGSMILL: Do you realise, Joe, that it's ten years already since Malcolm and I were writing *Brave Old World*, and you were doing those wonderful cartoons for it?

MAIDEN: Is it really? It doesn't seem anything like that. The war's telescoped everything, and it feels more like two than ten.

KINGSMILL: And yet I notice a mellowing in you which must have taken at least ten years to produce, unless your singularly winning smile misleads me. I still have some of those sketches you used to make of me in your spare moments. Johnson had his Joe Nollekens, and I have had my Joe Maiden, and when I remember "Kingsmill Wonders whether to join the Kipling Society or the Dickens Fellowship," I feel that Johnson missed or gained a good deal, according to the point of view.

Before parting, Kingsmill said that U.N.O. was amassing material for another book by Malcolm and himself. *Unonimity* wouldn't be a bad title, and would Joe be ready to do the drawings again? Joe, a steely glint behind his smile, said he would do his best.

GREENWICH

Taking a 53a bus at Whitehall, the travellers set out for Greenwich, each occupying a window seat, the one directly behind the other—comfort before comradeship. The dreary houses south of the river displeased Kingsmill, and after they had left the Old Kent Road and New Cross behind, he was about to condemn the expedition out of hand, but was stayed in his intention by Pearson indicating a terrace of houses built in the reign of William IV. How had Pearson come by his architectural knowledge? asked Kingsmill. What was it enabled him to place buildings within a reign of seven years? "It's observation, directed by unerring intuition," said Pearson. "It's the perfect correlation between the external fact and the internal feeling. The whole thing borders on the metaphysical, and I should confuse you further if I tried to clarify it; but Mozart playing like a master at the age of six gives you a clue."

The bus filled up, and three little girls got on, two of whom sat down by the side of Kingsmill and Pearson respectively. Kingsmill smiled down on his small neighbour, and Pearson, repelled by his friend's easy benevolence, asked his ditto if she would like his window seat. As he rose to give it her, there was a rush from the other side of the gangway, the third little girl took the seat vacated by her friend, and Pearson was left standing until the next stop.

Leaving the bus before it diverged to Blackheath, they walked towards the main street of Greenwich, where they discovered a roomy, dark-panelled Express Dairy. On emerging from it Kingsmill said that up to this point he condemned the expedition; it wasn't worth coming down to Greenwich to take tea at an Express Dairy, however commodious. But, he added, it was interesting to speculate whether this expedition, so paltry in its conception and hitherto so mean in its circumstances, was now about to justify itself. They walked down towards the Ship Hotel, which Pearson informed Kingsmill was one of the sights of Greenwich. "For well over a hundred years," he said, "from William Pitt's time onward, Ministers of the Crown and Leaders of the Opposition have sailed down the river for whitebait suppers at the Ship. Harris himself came here once as the guest of Randolph Churchill. That was in his unregenerate days, which he, but no one else, thought were over by forty; and wherever Frankie went in his pre-mystic period, everyone on the make went, too."

KINGSMILL: And of course it was the same in Elizabeth and James's days, when all the Randolphs and Frankies of the time were punting down the Thames for a smile or a kiss from Elizabeth or James.

Reaching the river, they paid their pennies to go on to the Wharf. Towards the west the chimneys of a great power-station were outlined against the sun which shone on the brimming water. The opposite shore was fringed with a narrow park through which some houses beyond were visible. "That's Woolwich Park," said Pearson, "where you and I sat last August and looked across at Greenwich and Shooters Hill above."

KINGSMILL: Eight months already! It's incredible. But surely that isn't Woolwich Park. It's too ragged, somehow, and I don't see the quay where the kids played and that space where the buses pulled up.

PEARSON: You don't see the quay where the kids played for the simple reason that it is entirely covered by that pyramid of barrels, which also hides the space where the buses pulled up. Even you must realise that barrels come and go, and that these have come and not yet gone.

KINGSMILL: All the same, the whole thing looks different to me.

PEARSON: Naturally, you fathead, as (*a*) it is different and (*b*) you're looking at it from a different angle.

KINGSMILL: All the same . . .

PEARSON: The whole thing looks different to you. Agreed.

Turning away, Pearson exclaimed "Good God! the Ship's been blitzed," and, pointing to the spot where the famous hotel had stood, sighed—"All, all are gone, the old familiar places."

Pearson took his friend along the river-side so as to give him a good view of the Naval College. They were admiring the group of buildings, and Kingsmill was wondering about what looked like a Regency house standing in the background and framed between the wings of the College, when an old man came along. "That's a fine house," said Kingsmill to him. "It's the Queen's House," replied the old man. "If you've never seen beautiful pictures in your life, you'll find them there." "Indeed?" "Ay, Nelson's relics." Pleased that an oldest inhabitant should be both informative and articulate, Kingsmill asked him the name of the Park across the river. The old man smiled—"We call it Scrap Iron Park. That's the Isle of Dogs over there, where everything's dumped. Used to be an island, but it's been joined up." "Then it isn't Woolwich Park?" queried Kingsmill. "Of course it ain't. Woolwich Park's down the river, round that bend. Getting on for two miles." Turning away from the Thames towards the Naval College, he was clearly on the point of opening out when Kingsmill, thanking him, said to Pearson that Mr. Jacobs would be growing impatient, and they really must hurry off.

As they went along, Pearson, taking in the salient points of the opposite shore, explained how and why Scrap Iron Park could in no circumstances be Woolwich Park, although, owing to the bend in the river which placed Greenwich in the same relation to both parks, their mistake had been natural.

Turning inland, they began to walk up towards Greenwich Park, and as they reached the entrance saw to their right at the end of a short street a pleasant-looking square. They diverged into it, and discovered it to consist of early nineteenth-century houses, once imposing but now sinking into decay. Three little girls were skipping in the road, one of them, in spite of her shabby clothes and grubby face, a very graceful and beautiful child, who told them the square was called Gloucester Circus. She and her companions skipped off towards the Park, and Pearson and Kingsmill followed, admiring the poise and springy step of the child, and feeling behind them the twilight gathering above the square.

They climbed to the top of the hill, passing some fine old mansions on their right, and, entering the Park, came out on the ridge, where they paused and looked down on the Thames, which wound between factories and cranes, buildings and docks, in two vast curves, and vanished out of sight on either hand. Before them, as they turned from the river, stretched the ancient Royal Park with its thousand-year oaks and thick, springy turf. "That avenue of trees," said Pearson, "must have led up to Elizabeth's Palace, and there's probably not one oak in that half-mile which wasn't three centuries old in Shakespeare's time."

Above the wall of the Park as they approached the Black-heath end they saw the new moon in the light evening sky. Beyond the Heath rose the dark mass of Shooters Hill, and along its western edge the ample Georgian houses loomed comfortably through the dusk.

ON GENTLEMEN

The wonderful weather since the middle of March proved too much for Pearson and Kingsmill on the afternoon of Saturday, April 6, and laying their work aside they set out for Regent's Park, which they reached on a bus. As they walked towards the Baker Street entrance Pearson said, "Not long ago I met a parson just about here. He was clothed in a cassock, and looked rather like a a friar—not that I've ever seen one. Accosting me with some severity, he said 'Can you tell me where St. Cyprian's Church is?'

" 'Sorry. I can't.'

" 'It's most extraordinary. You are the sixth person I've asked who doesn't know. Are there *no* Christians hereabouts?'

" 'I hope not,' I replied, and we parted curtly. I daresay he thought I was not a gentleman. I certainly thought he was not a Christian."

KINGSMILL: Are you a gentleman?

PEARSON: Yes, to the extent that I am not rude or overbearing to people who can't pay me back in kind. He showed himself so aggressively offensive that I realised my best efforts in that direction would still fall short of his. Yet I admit that a complete gentleman is never in any circumstances rude, and in this particular situation would have conveyed, quietly, his regret that there was a dearth of Christians thereabouts, and his hope that the priest's search would not continue to prove unrewarded.

KINGSMILL: A gentleman, in short, has all the qualities of a saint except saintliness. Like the saint, he does not react to other people's egotism, and therefore remains self-possessed and courteous, whatever the provocation. But unlike the saint he is not distressed by the shortcomings of others. A gentleman would have left your priest exactly as he found him. A saint would have left him feeling that there was a Christian about, and that the Christian wasn't the priest.

They paused on the bridge, and looking over the water towards the island with its tall trees, agreed that there was no lovelier scene in England. "This," said Pearson, "is the most beautiful park in London and I daresay in the universe. In Hyde Park and Kensington Gardens there's a feeling of being surrounded. One's conscious of being hemmed in by masses of houses on all sides. But here, though there are of course plenty of houses about, one doesn't feel enclosed, and over there on the north side the roads seem to be trekking straight for the country."

They went through Queen Mary's Garden, and as they turned down Broad Walk saw through the trees to their right the long line of Georgian terraces.

SIR WALTER SCOTT

PEARSON: Walter Scott had his last look at London from one of those terraces. He was on his way home to die and was staying with his son-in-law, Lockhart.

KINGSMILL: One doesn't associate him much with London, though John Buchan in his Life illustrates Scott's astonishing range of social intercourse by his London experiences, when on one evening he dined with George IV and on the following had supper with Harold Terry, the manager of Drury Lane Theatre. I'd have been more impressed if on the second evening he had looked in on

Blake to get a knotty point in the Prophetic Books cleared up.

PEARSON: Sad to think that no one nowadays reads Scott except you, me, and Sidney Webb.

KINGSMILL: Webb?

PEARSON: Yes. Kitty Muggeridge told me that she was staying with him not very long ago, and the following remarks passed between them—

"How do you occupy your time, Uncle Sidney?"

"I read one novel a day."

"What are you reading now?"

"I am reading the novels of Sir Walter Scott."

"Do you like them?"

"No."

KINGSMILL: Personally I'm extremely glad you persuaded me to re-read him during my post-plague period. After Shakespeare and Cervantes he's the richest, most human and humorous writer I know. Cuddie and his mother are second only to Don Quixote and Sancho, and being mother and son are even more poignantly funny.

PEARSON: I entirely agree, and *Old Mortality* also contains Balfour of Burley and Claverhouse, the finest fanatic and the finest free-lance soldier I've ever come across. And he's given us the two most life-like rulers, Louis XI and James I, the last-named being the most side-splitting comic in literature and the sole justification for the existence of politics.

KINGSMILL: Balzac says that Puritanism prevented Scott from drawing life-like women. Admittedly, Balzac was unhampered by Puritanism, but he hasn't a woman who's worth mentioning in comparison with Catharine Seyton.

PEARSON: The most adorable, delectable, mischievous

little wretch—and to think she's thrown away on one of those dreary prigs whom poor old Scott imagined united all the manly virtues.

KINGSMILL: Those heroes of his embodied his daydreams, in which he performed prodigies of valour, faced insuperable odds, and took every kind of risk without any kind of tremor. But reality will break through, and the amusing thing about his heroes is that he can't refrain from endowing them with a goodly portion of the canny self-interest which kept Scott himself from being needlessly heroic where his own affairs were concerned. When I was reading *Old Mortality* I was considerably less surprised than Scott appears to be at the general view among the Covenanting rebels that Henry Morton had gone over to the enemy. As Morton ends up under the special protection of Claverhouse, while his old associates are being tortured or hanged, I don't see what other view was open to them. Nor does Quentin Durward quite realise my idea of the Chevalier Bayard when he complies with Louis XI's instructions that he shall stand behind a curtain with a loaded arquebus, ready at a signal to discharge the same at a gentleman who is under the impression that he is attending a reconciliation banquet with the King.

PEARSON: And when Scott at last, in *The Fortunes of Nigel*, does attempt to draw a life-like Scottish youth, he's so divided in his purpose that on one page Lord Nigel is making his out-of-pocket expenses by rooking simpletons in a gambling den, and on another is flourishing his sword and spitting defiance at the all-powerful minion of the king.

KINGSMILL: And his divided purpose comes out even more absurdly over Nigel's marriage. Having screwed himself up to show a Scottish aristocrat falling in love with a citizen's daughter—and a most enchanting kid she is, second only to Catharine Seyton—he is so overwhelmed by the horror of what he has done that beyond mentioning that the bride and bridegroom were present he completely ignores their existence in the chapter devoted to their wedding.

CONSTABLE'S COUNTRY

Depressed by the cloudy sky in the early morning of Wednesday, April 24, Kingsmill rang up Pearson to ask him if he thought it fine enough for their journey to the Constable country, and Pearson said it would clear up later. The train for Manningtree left Liverpool Street Station at 10.30, and while waiting for it to start the travellers, who had corner seats in a first-class carriage, looked appreciatively out of the window.

PEARSON: This station is undiluted mid-Victorian horror. It's gloomy, grimy, claustrophobic, and furtive.

KINGSMILL: I always associate it with the black-coated, well-whiskered murderers of the sixties and seventies— say, a bank manager from Lowestoft, a lay preacher whose first wife, supposed to have gone abroad, is fished out from under the rose-bush at the bottom of the garden some three years after his marriage to a pretty young Sunday school teacher.

PEARSON: The only other station at all like this one is King's Cross, and, oddly enough, both of them feed the Eastern Counties. Puritanism, I suppose. It's essentially

East Coast—Calvinists from the Low Countries, and Huguenots from France, and such home products as Wycliffe, Wesley and Cromwell.

As the train passed through Stratford, Kingsmill said he presumed this was Chaucer's Stratford atte Bowe where the Wife of Bath had learnt her French—quite an amusing comment when Chaucer made it, no doubt, but hardly worth the many repetitions during the intervening centuries. Apparently even Shakespeare thought it was too much of a chestnut to give to one of his clowns, though it must have been a near thing with Touchstone.

Until the train had left London and the suburbs well behind, the weather still gave the travellers cause for anxiety, but as they reached the gentle undulations of Essex, Pearson in his character of prophet was able to cry out "I told you so. The perfect Constable day—bright clouds on the horizon and blue sky above!" The old cottages and well-hedged fields and neighbouring skylines stirred early memories in both of them. "There's a lot in a remark Brian once made to me," Kingsmill said, "to the effect that old associations are more keenly stimulated by places one has not seen before than by places one revisits." "That's very true," said Pearson. "And I suppose the reason is that when one revisits a place there's usually a clash between what one remembers and what one sees."

After a brief pause Kingsmill enquired "How old are hedges?"

"As with trees, it depends on their age, but if you had put your query in a rational form I would have replied: Hedges are constantly being renovated by clipping— hedging, if you like. Therefore hedges, broadly speaking, consist of the younger sprigs of the old roots, the roots themselves being pushed farther and farther underground. So these hedges we are looking at are probably from twenty to thirty years old, but the parent stems, now underground, are anything from two to three hundred years. Not more than three, because hedges as a general feature of the landscape came in with the enclosure of the common land."

Some little way beyond Colchester, Pearson, looking out of the window, remarked that this was typical Suffolk scenery—a broad-bottomed valley enclosed by gently sloping hills. The train reached Manningtree, and the travellers were a little disconcerted at the large number of naval ratings, with an officer or two, who were getting out with them. Was this a mob of Constable fans? they wondered, and were greatly relieved on seeing them disappear into a train on a side line, bound, apparently, for Harwich.

PEARSON: "Roasted Manningtree ox"–that is my only association with this junction to Harwich. That's what Prince Hal called Falstaff, and I need hardly say that none of the innumerable professors who batten on Shakespeare has thrown the least light on it. At a venture I should say that oxen were roasted at Manningtree.

Kingsmill meanwhile enquired of the ticket collector if there was a train about six. "Where to?" asked the ticket collector. "Back," said Kingsmill. "Back where?" asked the ticket collector. "London," said Kingsmill. "Yes," said the ticket collector, who went on to suggest, perhaps in his own interests, that they had better return from Colchester.

It was a beautiful day as they left the station and caught a bus which was just coming up. A muddy tidal river stretched away on either hand between fresh water-meadows, and the road beyond curved away from the old houses of Manningtree up the slope which they had seen from the train, running for two or three miles between hedges and blossoming trees. Descending at the far end of East Bergholt, they walked back through the village and paused outside the churchyard to look at the gravestones. A lame elderly man hobbling by stopped to say "Their heads don't ache now," but rather spoilt the effect by claiming to have known the three persons commemorated on the gravestones they were reading, all of whom had died in the 1830's. And when he went on to attribute to one of the deceased a quip, the humour of which had begun to pall on Pearson and Kingsmill in their early teens, they were confirmed in their long-standing suspicion that rural integrity and rustic wisdom were urban myths.

Pearson having discriminated the various architectural periods of East Bergholt Church, they turned off the main thoroughfare and took the road to Flatford Mill. Below them spread the valley immortalised by Constable, Dedham Church in the distance.

PEARSON: This isn't at all how I imagined his country. There's a cosiness in his pictures which is absent here. This is all much more open. It's beautiful, but it's different.

KINGSMILL: And that winding river, which must be the Stour, somehow doesn't recall him.

PEARSON: Mill-ponds, yes. Winding rivers, no.

The road narrowed and dipped steeply down between tall, over-arching trees through which the sunlight poured in narrow shafts. It recalled Savernake Forest to them both, the difference, Pearson said, being that this was a side aisle in a cathedral, and that had been the main one.

They came to the little wooden bridge over the river.

By its side was a sixteenth-century thatched cottage where teas were served on a terrace bordered by flowers, yellow and blue and white, which were reflected in the water; and farther down-stream they could see Flatford Mill. Retracing their steps a short distance, they had lunch in a farmhouse among the trees. "How Constable would have loved the sunshine on those leaves," said Kingsmill. "He says somewhere that what he aimed at in his pictures was light and dews and breezes, and that he cared less for autumnal tints than for the exhilarating freshness of the spring."

Pearson: But there was nothing he couldn't see beauty in. He once declared that he had never seen an ugly thing in his life. As he was happy in himself, he was in harmony with his surroundings–hence his saying that no great painter had ever been eccentric.

Kingsmill: And as he wasn't eccentric, he was ignored. He'd hardly any fame in his own day, and suggested the reason himself when in reference to the current taste for spectacular melodramatic painting he quoted that passage from the Book of Kings which really contains all that need be said about art of any kind–"A great and strong wind rent the mountains, and brake in pieces the rocks before the Lord; but the Lord was not in the wind: And after the wind an earthquake; but the Lord was not in the earthquake: And after the earthquake a fire; but the Lord was not in the fire: And after the fire a still small voice."

Looking at Flatford Mill from across the river, they agreed that this was the scene which they had expected to find, warm and compact, with harmonious effects of light and shade. On their way to examine the Mill from the other side, they sought for examples of the still small voice, and found them in Beethoven, Wordsworth and Constable, as opposed to the winds and earthquakes and fires of Wagner, Shelley and Turner; "for," said Pearson, "Beethoven *is* ultimately the still small voice of the Lord."

They walked towards Dedham by the winding Stour. Across the river the rooks were nesting in the tall elms, their discordant croaking seeming to complete the serenity of the scene. Sometimes a pair of wild duck whirred above the water, settled with a splash and floated gently along. In a meadow on the far side two horses were meditatively licking each other. Leaving the river, they crossed a field containing about a hundred bullocks, who stared balefully at the travellers, as though wishing they were strong enough to do them an injury. The fine tower of Dedham Church appeared above the high trees surrounding it. They entered the village and found themselves in the most beautiful street they had ever seen, nearly every house perfect of its kind and period; and again, as in Richmond, they had the feeling that a past England, unseen in their youth, was now disclosing itself. As Pearson preceded Kingsmill into the church, he said "Every church in Suffolk is a cathedral. It was from these vast East Anglian edifices that Cobbett inferred the populous agricultural communities of the Middle Ages. G. K. C. made a lot of this discovery, the effect of which he did not spoil by adding that people in those days were fined for not going to church, a regulation which, if it were now enforced, would require an Albert Hall in every parish."

They seated themselves; the organ was playing and the church was filled with the perfume of the spring flowers brought for the Easter celebration. Wandering round the churchyard, they looked over a wall into a neighbouring paddock, which turned out to be what Pearson, in the course of his storm-tossed life, had always longed for—a small field of untended grass with a large tree in the centre under which he would recline in a deckchair, listening to the chimes and admiring the creamy blossoms bubbling on a tall pear tree nearby.

COLCHESTER

They walked up to the end of the village street, enjoying the houses on the way, and especially taken with the last two, the clean light brick of the eighteenth-century one contrasting with the rich red of the seventeenth century. After tea at The Cottage Corner, they took the bus to Colchester, of which town they knew nothing except that Fairfax had captured it in the Civil War and, though on other occasions chivalrous enough, had executed the Royalist leaders, perhaps to show Cromwell that the Lord's mercies were not restricted to *him*. The travellers had pictured a commonplace town in a flat country, and found instead an ancient and formidable town whose great streets climbed up from the valley and met on the high ridge which constituted the main thoroughfare, such a place as Bunyan imagined for Mansoul, the citadel beleaguered by all the hosts of hell. Nevertheless, they took a bus to the station, wondering how long they would have to wait for a train; but as they reached the platform they saw the London express approaching, and realised that the Lord's mercies were not restricted to Cromwell and Fairfax.

POWER POLITICS

On May Day, Kingsmill, who had recently moved to a flat in Westbourne Terrace, from the bathroom of which he was able to watch the sun rising over Arbuckle Avenue, leaving the house to join Pearson at the Club, came upon a dispute between two small groups of boys. One of the groups had entered the enclosure between the terrace and the main road, and the spokesman of the other group was shouting "You mustn't come in here." "You mind your own business where I come in," retorted the leader of the invading group; but, seeing himself outnumbered, he withdrew slowly with his forces.

FAG-ENDS

After lunch Pearson and Kingsmill crossed Hungerford Bridge on the way to Hampton Court. It was a fresh spring day, and the City spires against the blue sky looked intensely white above the white span of Waterloo Bridge. Descending the steps on the far side, they passed a shabbily dressed man who under the shelter of a wall was fanning a pile of loose tobacco spread out on a newspaper. "An odd job," said Pearson. "That fellow must spend his spare time looking for fag-ends in the gutter, and then when he's collected enough he removes the paper, and that fanning process must be to blow away any remaining fragments.

What's left over he doubtless takes to some tobacconist who either reconverts it into cigarettes or sells it as pipe tobacco.''

KINGSMILL: All the same, I'm much too fond of my pipe to give it up. But what do you think he makes a week?

PEARSON: A good week might bring him in £2.

KINGSMILL: I can't see a fag-end anywhere—Oh, there's one, but it would take me a month to collect his pile, and I can't believe he picks up £2 worth in a week.

PEARSON: This wouldn't be one of his hunting-grounds. His best pitches, I should say, are outside restaurants, theatres and cinemas, where people both going in and coming out discard their cigarettes, even if they are only half smoked—a relic of the times when smoking was frowned on.

KINGSMILL: But smoking used to be tolerated in the open, so why should people throw away their cigarettes on emerging into the street?

PEARSON: Because any sudden change of surroundings revives the old taboo.

They went on, their eyes darting in every direction, and each calling to the other when they sighted a stump; but as they drew near Waterloo Station the fag-ends multiplied so much that, in the interests of their expedition, they agreed to desist.

HAMPTON COURT

When the train halted at Clapham Junction, Pearson said "This was Oscar's calvary, probably on that very platform, where the trains from Wandsworth come in. There he stood for half-an-hour in the November rain, ill, handcuffed and in convict dress, surrounded by a jeering crowd."

KINGSMILL: And it was only eight months since he stood before a cheering crowd at the first night of *The Importance of Being Earnest*. Life is really very intimidating. He had always wanted to be the centre of public notice, and here was life still attending to his wants. I wonder what the poor chap looked like. He was a big, fat boy, stuffing himself with cream tarts in the days of his success, but here he must have looked cowed and bewildered, like a boy who has been bullied and crouches away from his tormentors.

Leaving the train at Kingston, they caught a bus for Hampton Court, where they alighted at the Green and walked back to Bushey Park. On the way they noticed a dog who had poked his head through the rails of a first-floor veranda and was looking down at them with a yearning expression, as though at long last his search for sympathy and understanding was about to be rewarded. They could not help bursting into laughter. The dog's mood instantly changed to one of rage; he broke into furious barking, and they could still hear him venting his bitter resentment as they turned into the park, where the chestnuts in the mile-long avenue were in full bloom.

After tea they entered the grounds of Hampton Court and passing the front of Wolsey's Palace came out on the river-side. As they walked along, Pearson, drawing his friend's attention to a portion of the Palace with old tiles and latticed attics, surmised that Wolsey must have built that bit first as a river residence, and the rest had been added gradually.

KINGSMILL: It's curious that, although this marvellous building proves Wolsey to have been in the front rank of looters, it's very difficult to think of a cardinal being no better than a lay looter. One feels that someone who is frequently mentioning Christ cannot be entirely indifferent to Christ's point of view.

PEARSON: I agree, and have the same feeling whenever I'm reading about Richelieu. This doesn't apply to Mazarin, I suppose because he is an Italian, and it is really asking too much of one's subconsciousness to expect it to have any illusions about Rome.

Retracing their steps, they passed through the central entrance of Wolsey's Palace into the courtyards beyond.

KINGSMILL: I suppose Wolsey built all this so that posterity should talk about him, as indeed we're doing at this moment, though not perhaps along the lines he would prefer.

PEARSON: It's the most certain way in which men of action can perpetuate their memory. Not artists themselves, they are in a position to bribe or threaten artists into directing the attention of posterity to themselves. Hence the Pyramids, hence Fati-pur-Sikri, hence the Taj Mahal, hence Versailles, hence Hitler's Berlin, hence Mussolini's Rome, and hence William III's addition to Hampton Court, which we are now entering. As you can see, it's Wren at his best. Look at that superb courtyard, and the high perfectly spaced windows.

KINGSMILL: It's very fine, but a bit too formal, I think, and hasn't the charm of his more homely architecture or the poetic atmosphere of the Tudor palace, which may be largely due to literary associations.

As they came out in front of Wren's palace, they saw on either hand the beds of many-coloured tulips, a present from the Dutch Government to the English people, and beyond the formal lawn a long stretch of ornamental water bordered by tall trees, a vista of great beauty, probably inspired by Versailles, but less ostentatious and more friendly.

Leaning on a parapet, they watched the ducks and fish, Pearson inclining to the view that a wild duck in tame surroundings is the most fortunate of living creatures, and adding that he would like to be one if he had to be reincarnated, Kingsmill admitting that, against reason, he could not help feeling that to be half in and half out of water must be chilly, and that therefore he would prefer to be a fish. These points decided, they walked along an avenue and sat on a bench overlooking the river.

PEARSON: I wonder if Charles I and Cromwell, during all the conferences here which so got on the nerves of the Puritan extremists, ever wandered arm in arm along this river-bank. No one could be more charming than Cromwell when it was his cue, and Charles, who loved Hampton, must often have felt that the worst was over, and could never have suspected that it was still to come.

KINGSMILL: What unnecessary trouble these men of action go to in order to visit famous and beautiful places. It took Hitler eighteen years of toil and strain, the support of eighty-five million people, and the co-operation of an enormous army and air force to get to Paris. Napoleon went through much the same process in order to reach Berlin; and whereas you and I have arrived at Hampton Court without any opposition in well under two hours, and on a total budget of less than ten shillings, Cromwell had to hack his bloody way to this beautiful scene through all the lanes and villages of his native land.

PEARSON: Men of action are under the illusion that happiness is outside themselves, and everyone who has that illusion would be a man of action if he had the necessary guts and go. As you know, I have been in the unpleasant position of having to masquerade as a man of action, and while in that role was misunderstood by my friend Harold, who accused me of laziness because I was perfectly content to do nothing, and wished everyone else to do likewise. I remember one day a few years ago, when I was sitting in the garden of Goldhurst Terrace, I heard my next-door neighbour say "If I had my life over again, I'd live it very differently." My impulse, not strong enough to issue in action, was to call out "If you had your life over again, you'd be the same bloody fool you are now." As he wished to be different, it was obvious that whatever he was he would never wish to be the same, and therefore must have been a man of action or wanted to be one—more probably the latter, as he was living next door to me. I myself would be quite content to live my present life once more. With the exception of my early school days, which I hated so much that on the very rare occasions when I have a nightmare I imagine myself back in my preparatory school, I would re-live everything. In fact, I find life much too short. I could do with five lives: one for love and friendship, another for eating and drinking, a third for literature and music, a fourth for architecture and nature, and a fifth for creation and contemplation.

KINGSMILL: If I had my life over again, I'd use fewer commas. I was looking at one of my books the other day and was surprised at the unnecessary commas it contained. But so far as semi-colons are concerned, I have nothing to regret.

ON CADS

Kingsmill arrived at the Club on Wednesday, May 8, to find Pearson still flushed after interchanging opinions on success with a fellow member. "He asked me," said Pearson, "whether I considered that I had made a success of life. I gave an unqualified 'Yes,' which led him to suppose that I had made a mint of money. I was then compelled to inform him that in relation to success there are four types of cad. The highest type thinks that success depends on the number of women a man can pop into bed with; highest because, after all, there is some reciprocity and humanity in the business. The next-best type identifies success with titles, public honours and so forth; and that is bearable because it implies a more or less harmless form of vanity. Next comes the cad who judges success by the amount of power a man can exercise over his fellow-creatures, which at least implies that he is aware of other people's existence. But, and at this point I favoured him with a truly baleful glare, the really hell-spawned cad is he who estimates success in terms of money. It was my intention to conclude with a few words on true success, but I found that he had gone."

REGENT STREET

After lunch they took a taxi to Regent's Park, the starting point of their predetermined walk down Euston Road. As they drove along, Kingsmill asked Pearson if he could remember how long ago it was since the old Regent Street was taken down.

PEARSON: Regent Street was practically unaltered since the time of the Regent until the early 1920's, when all these five-storeyed erections were run up by a number of cads who computed success by money and turned what was

Regent St., 1823

primarily a work of art and secondarily a shopping centre into what is primarily a shopping centre and secondarily nothing at all. From Carlton House at the bottom of Lower Regent Street right up to the north end of Regent's Park, Nash had planned and executed a magnificent royal road, the finest in the world, and here is this conglomeration of concrete planked down in the middle of it. And, mind, it's Crown property. People have been knighted for preserving architectural masterpieces, but no one has been unkinged for destroying them.

Leaving the taxi, they passed Holy Trinity Church, opposite Great Portland Street station, and Pearson said he had often wondered about the outside pulpit on the western wall. Why was it there? Did anyone preach from it? And could he be heard, or was he drowned by the traffic? Probably, said Kingsmill, it dated from at least two hundred years back, when there was no traffic thereabouts and out-of-door preaching was in use. After they had debated the matter for some time, they approached the church, and discovered that the pulpit had been erected to the memory of the Reverend William Cadman, vicar from 1859 to 1891. Turning away, they were stopped by a foreigner who asked to be directed to Stamford Hill. Pearson said it was S.E., but the foreigner said it was N. or N.W., and, ignoring Kingsmill's suggestion that he should enquire at Great Portland Street station, left them. As they went on their way, the travellers debated the whereabouts of Stamford Hill, Pearson still holding out for S.E., Kingsmill disposed to back the foreigner. Crossing over to Warren Street station, Kingsmill enquired at the booking-office, but the girl did not know. "Well, anyway," he said, on rejoining his friend, "I used to come along this road with my nurse fifty years ago. That, at least, is certain, whatever may be thought of my views on outdoor pulpits and how to get to Stamford Hill. And I used often to dream about that Maple's warehouse over there. It's gloomy enough now, but in the middle nineties, when there were still black fogs and even the trees in the park were dark with soot, it was quite nightmarish. Let's have a look at it."

Crossing Tottenham Court Road to the north side of

Euston Road, they entered a dim yard which seemed enveloped in a sodden twilight. "A real fragment of Victorian London, the City of Dreadful Night," said Kingsmill as they emerged. "It was still going strong in the nineties, and though I don't suppose I was often out late at the age of five or six, I can remember the flaring gas-jets outside the butchers' shops in Hampstead Road, and I've a kind of composite picture, which may owe something to later experience and reading, of this road at that time— shabby, ragged men and women, the men sometimes reeling, the women tipsy and high-voiced, large battered picture hats wobbling on their heads."

PEARSON: How completely changed the Euston Road  is now, even from 1905 when I first knew it. Then the gardens on each side came right down to what is now the road, but they've been pushed back on this side, and built over on that, in spite of which the road is infinitely more cheerful. That may be partly due to having been widened, but it's much more due to the fact that the grimy, sooty gardens bordering it deepened instead of lightening the gloom. With the advent of electricity the country came back to town. I am aware that in some quarters of London buildings predominate, but much of the town nowadays is woodland interspersed with houses.

KINGSMILL: All the same, those buildings over there

which have been planted on Endsleigh Gardens always give me a slight pang. The gardens themselves were all you say in the way of grime and soot, but as I used to play there I was surprised and annoyed in the early 1920's when they put up those houses. In fact, for a long time I had a feeling they were only there provisionally, and that the gardens still existed, and could, if they felt like it, re-emerge.

Diverging from Euston Road, they passed No. 5, Endsleigh Gardens, Kingsmill's old home.

KINGSMILL: We were an earnest and upright body of men in these parts when I was young. There was my father, of course, at No. 5, where the expansion of his tourist business, which was intricately inter-related with his religious activities, was gradually driving his family into the upper storeys. Round the corner was the Reverend Hugh Price Hughes, my godfather, a fore-front fighter in the cause of social purity and a fiery Welsh orator who just outdistanced Stead in popular esteem as the whip that had scourged the adulterous Parnell out of public life. At No. 15, I think, was Sir Percy Bunting, whom I remember as a stoutish, mild, rather remote little man, editor of the *Contemporary Review*, a monthly journal which dealt with the social evil, as it was then called, in a manner which might not have seemed very real to the prostitutes wandering along on the far side of the gardens. His sister, Mrs. Amos, who looked like a handsomer George Eliot, was a much more energetic character, and once on Paddington platform struck a Guards officer who had been guilty of seduction. Somewhere in the middle distance, but I do not remember him personally, lived Mr. Algernon Coote, founder and secretary of the National Vigilance Association, which arranged that girls coming from the provinces for employment in London should be met on arrival, steered through the multitudinous perils of the street, and penned in a fold where liberty of action was restricted to attending church on Sunday. Yet here I am, at the age of fifty-six, not suffering, so far as I know, from any incurable disease.

PEARSON: And with Vestryman Shaw then running the Borough of St. Pancras, it's a wonder you're not a dipsomaniac too.

THE DOOR

Standing in Bloomsbury Square in front of Lord Chesterfield's house, Kingsmill regretted he had had no notion, when he was writing on Johnson, that the door from which he had been repulsed by Chesterfield's lackeys was still in existence, and added that it was a pity Pearson had withheld this piece of information until two or three years ago.

PEARSON: During Chesterfield's lifetime this house stood on the edge of the country. Lord Mansfield lived on the other side of the present square, and that was probably the only building Chesterfield saw when he looked from his windows. It was in and out of that door, facing the square, that Chesterfield went, and it was no doubt from this side door that Johnson was repulsed. An impressive place. That inhuman block over there dwarfs it now, but it must have been one of the most imposing mansions in eighteenth-century London.

KINGSMILL: I remember pointing it out to William Gerhardi in the summer of '44, on the way to *Punch*, where I was fire-watching. From here we went to Johnson's house in Gough Square, and as we paused in front of it I told William that this was the place where Johnson had toiled on his Dictionary. For a few moments we stood in silence, William grave and understanding. Then I noticed a sudden glint in his eye, and knew that trouble was hatching. "It is a very fine house," he said impatiently. "It is just as fine as Chesterfield's. I do not see why Chesterfield should have helped Johnson with his rent when Johnson was not helping Chesterfield with his."

Pearson and Kingsmill, continuing on their way, crossed the square into Great Russell Street, and as they passed the British Museum were conscious of a slight nostalgia for the years when they had frequented its reading-room, and a keen hope that those years would not return. "The Museum is a good rendez-vous, anyhow," said Kingsmill. "You can't miss it, though I remember Lance Sieveking, whom I was meeting there, writing to me 'I shall be in front of the Museum. You will know me because I shall have boots on.' "

THE CANADIAN BOAT SONG

Pausing at 90, Great Russell Street, Kingsmill said to Pearson "Why not look up Hamish? If he's in, he won't have time to get out." Pearson demurred, but Kingsmill had already entered and was asking the reception clerk to tell Mr. Hamilton that Hesketh Pearson was below. "It's all right," he said, going out into the passage and beckoning to Pearson. "He wants to see us."

They mounted to the first floor, and Hamish Hamilton's face, momentarily distorted at the sight of Kingsmill, partially composed itself as Pearson loomed through the curtain. "Have you come to buy any copies of *Skye High*?" he asked genially. "As many as you've got," said Pearson meaningly. Hamish, not availing himself of this opportunity to promise a speedy reprint, smiled, and introduced them to Mr. Cass Canfield, Chairman of Harper's. After a pleasant talk, in the course of which an occasional spasm passed over Hamish's face, they left, promising to call again.

KINGSMILL: Did you notice the fleeting look of agony on Hamish's face while we were talking? I suppose in the ten years since *Skye High* he must occasionally have dreamed that you and I were sitting opposite him again, putting up some hellish proposition in comparison with which even our Scottish tour would have seemed a relatively well-weighed and advantageous enterprise. So perhaps those spasms meant that he was wondering whether he was awake or asleep.

PEARSON: "And he in dreams beholds the Hebrides."

SOHO

As they crossed Oxford Street on their way south, Pearson remarked "This is a street I always cross. I never walk a yard farther along it than is strictly necessary. It is a street totally devoid of atmosphere; it might be in any other town in the world; and it's always crammed with shoppers.''

KINGSMILL: Probably that is why I connect it with those lions and tigers filled with bran which one had when a kid. They must have been sold hereabouts, and I remember we often came along this street, no doubt because our nurse loved the shops.

PEARSON: Anyhow, for me Oxford Street only becomes human when it becomes Holborn. Can you remember how Holborn struck your nurse? Not? A pity. Now here *is* a place with atmosphere. Not only is Soho a perfect specimen of Queen Anne architecture, but its associations with that period have been utterly ruined by the torrent of French, Russian, and Italian refugees and revolutionaries who flowed into it during the nineteenth century and poured out of it in the twentieth in order to occupy the highest positions in Italy and Russia, though not yet, thank God, in France. Curious that as their chief use over here was to provide us whom they loathed with cheap and varied meals, they should have reduced their own dear countrymen to famine level.

KINGSMILL: I was remarking to Malcolm not long ago how strange it was that Francis Thompson should have had the same experience as De Quincey, who was befriended by a prostitute in one of these streets. Under cross-examination I had to admit that De Quincey's *Confessions* was Thompson's favourite reading before he came to London, that in

32, Soho Square, (1767)

imitation of De Quincey Thompson took to opium,
and that he was not only befriended by a prostitute
on reaching London, but, like De Quincey, lost sight of
her almost at once and was never able to find her
again. Need I add that I was very rapidly compelled to
concede that Francis Thompson's prostitute existed only
in his imagination; and, after a rather longer struggle, I
allowed it was not very probable a prostitute would have
befriended De Quincey. But I would not agree with
Malcolm that, if she had, she would never have got out of
his clutches. There I stood firm.

ALBERT GRANT, ESQ., M.P.

On reaching Leicester Square Kingsmill asked Pearson if
he knew the statue of Albert Grant. No, said Pearson;
so Kingsmill led him to the centre of the Square and
pointed at an Elizabethan figure in doublet and hose who
was resting his elbow on a volume and trying to look
thoughtful.

PEARSON: But, damn it, that's Shakespeare! I've known
it as long as I've known London. Everyone knows it. It's
the most familiar statue in the world.

KINGSMILL: Well, let's read the inscription. That should
settle it.

Approaching the statue they read—

This enclosure was purchased, laid out and decorated
as a garden by ALBERT GRANT, Esq., M.P. and con-

veyed by him on 2nd July, 1874, to the Metropolitan Board of Works to be preserved for ever for the free use and enjoyment of the public.

KINGSMILL: As you see, there's no mention of Shakespeare anywhere on the monument; and I therefore infer that the man up there is Albert Grant, a scrupulous company promoter, whose maiden name, I understand, was Gottheimer. Have you any comments to make?
PEARSON: None.

JAMES THOMSON

While walking down Euston Road, they had decided to fulfil their promise to Graham Greene and round off the afternoon with a visit to Vauxhall Bridge Road to discover if James Thomson's house was still standing. So, on leaving Albert Grant, they hailed a taxi and asked the driver to take them to number 240. The driver, evidently as unacquainted with Vauxhall Bridge Road as themselves, crawled down the left-hand side peering listlessly at the passing houses until the travellers decided to ease his strain by getting out.

"There's 246," said Kingsmill. "And there's 242," cried Pearson. Next to 242 stood a large modern block, and on perceiving that it was numbered 232–240, the travellers realised that Thomson's lodging-house had vanished even more completely than Graham Greene's other old-world haunt, Arbuckle Avenue. GLYMIEL JELLY ran across the whole frontage of the building, and underneath in smaller lettering *For Soft White Hands Whatever the Weather*.

KINGSMILL: There was only one kind of weather for poor Thomson, and it wasn't the care of his hands he worried about during it. I remember a description of him coming into a bar from the slush and darkness outside, his clothes looking as if he had slept in them, and on his feet worn-out carpet slippers, through which his bare skin showed. I wonder how he reached such a state. He himself believed it was because the girl he loved died before they could be married, and his lines on her are intensely moving, even though one may feel they don't contain the real explanation—

> You would have saved me from the desert sands,
> Bestrewn with bleaching bones. . . .

PEARSON: One can see from 242 what 240 was like. Those squalid three-storeyed houses, dingy enough at the beginning of Queen Victoria's reign but unspeakably repulsive after forty years of the filth of industrial London— those hissing gas-jets, the ghastliest illumination ever invented, giving a spectral reality to the cramped rooms with their mean furniture and gruesome ornaments.

KINGSMILL: A sodden, hopeless town, with no sky or stars above it, but only the impenetrable fog which closes over his City of Dreadful Night, and is felt in every stanza of the poem.

PEARSON :

> O melancholy Brothers, dark, dark, dark!
> O battling in black floods without an ark!
> O spectral wanderers of unholy night!
> My soul hath bled for you these sunless years,
> With bitter blood-drops running down like tears:
> O, dark, dark, dark, withdrawn from joy and light.

"What a delightful high street!" Pearson exclaimed as he and Kingsmill reached Gravesend on the following Wednesday. Hurrying down to the river, they caught a glimpse of a fresh green shore opposite and a steamer sailing Londonwards, and were back at the Maidstone and District Depot in time for the bus to Cobham. As they drove along under a bright sky through winding roads over a well-cultivated table-land, Pearson said "This country is not a bit as I pictured it from *Great Expectations*—a grey, marshy land with convict hulks looming through the mist."

Dismounting in Cobham, they went into the Leather Bottle, the chief rural shrine of the Dickens faith, and found the walls of the inn congested with photographs, prints, and framed newspaper reports relating to Dickens, and an endless gallery of the novelist's characters, not only Phiz and the other original illustrators, but also later artists, and sketches of the actors who had played in stage adaptations.

"This is worse than Stratford-on-Avon, because more concentrated," Pearson cried. "What have we here? It looks like our Liverpool Street Station murderer. Oh, it's Dickens reading *Dombey and Son*. Here he is again, all his murders behind him, in the part of the Gadshill squire, surrounded by his family.

KINGSMILL: The rest of the caste look apprehensive. They're not playing up, and they know it. I daresay he sacked the lot when he had the result before him. Let's hear what the *New York Herald* has to say about him. It's dated February 1842, I see, and opens as follows:—'The arrival of Dickens is a new era in the history of mankind. Since the creation of the world and the fall of man nothing like it has taken place.' Well, that's equally true of this issue of the *New York Herald*.

They went into lunch. On the dining-room wall hung a large photograph of Mary Anderson, a famous stage beauty of the eighties, and Pearson heard a lady whisper to her companion "I wonder if that's Ellen Ternan."

"A fruitful notion, that," murmured Pearson to Kingsmill, "and points the way to an ideal selection of pictures for a Dickens shrine. Four would be sufficient: one of Shakespeare, one of Thackeray, one of Ellen Ternan, and I should have no objection to the fourth being that one in the corridor of Beerbohm Tree as Fagin."

THE ROAD TO ROCHESTER

After lunch they walked through the village of Cobham, and as they reached the Park saw to their left a high green glade suffused with sunshine, and to their right miles of open country with hardly a house in sight, proof, said Pearson, of what he was always remarking, that England is a nightmare for anyone who suffers from agoraphobia, and a paradise for those who, while not averse from humanity, like it commodiously spaced. Bearing left when they reached the Park, they went down to Cobham Hall, a fine Elizabethan building, and passing through the gate asked a young man if they were right for Gadshill. They were, he said, but added that it was not a right of way, and that he was getting rather tired of the numerous excursionists who treated the Cobham estate as a convenient short cut. Would he prefer them to turn back, the travellers enquired? As they were there, he conceded, they had better carry on; and in answer to a question from Kingsmill informed them that it was six miles to Gadshill. "He's doubled the distance," said Pearson as they proceeded. "I've done the walk before, so I know." Kingsmill wondered if the family was still in residence, and if their rather obstructive informant was connected with it. Rounding a corner, they saw a placard in front of the building bearing the words *Cobham Estate Limited*, and inferred that they had been speaking to one of the minds behind that enterprise.

They walked on through beautiful lanes, the woods on either hand full of bluebells and here and there a clearing where the trees had been felled and stacked. Kingsmill wondered what all the wood was stacked for, and Pearson, loth to withhold information whether he possessed it or not, replied that it was for wood purposes. A house standing back from the road attracted them, and Pearson exclaimed "Look at that white house! I'd like to take it at once and clear out the owner lock, stock, but not barrel; then I'd be at peace at last." Far below to their left, beyond meadows yellow with broom sinking to a wooded spur, stretched bright green fields towards a wide river which lay pale blue and still in the sunshine, two or three fishing-vessels on its surface and a steamer hardly moving. The scene was so remote from the labour and stress of life, from all the associations of great waterways, they could hardly believe it was the Thames at which they were looking.

Emerging into the London–Rochester road, they walked along it, hoping for a bus to pick them up, and reached

Gadshill Place just as one came into view. Rushing Kingsmill through the gate, Pearson exclaimed "There it is!", and rushed him out again. When they had settled themselves on top of the bus Pearson continued "And here is Sir John Falstaff's Inn, and before us is the scene of the famous robbery." "I fancy," said Kingsmill, "that if Dickens had been in residence here at the time, he would have got Falstaff into the Fleet at the beginning of *Henry IV Part I* instead of at the close of *Henry IV Part II*."

ROCHESTER

After tea they strolled round the Cathedral and sat for a while in the pleasant old garden on the south side, with its crumbling walls. Rambling on, they passed through a park called The Vines, looked in at a field where a cricket match was being played, and went up the hill to St. Margaret's Church, where they leant against the graveyard wall and looked down on the shining Medway which curved away to the west and vanished into the Kentish countryside. On their way back, as they reached Minor Canon Row, a perfect Queen Anne terrace marred by green wooden railings, they encountered an elderly clergyman of a most taking aspect who, noticing their topographical curiosity, smiled and asked them if they were strangers. They told him how much they were enjoying the old buildings in the neighbourhood of the Cathedral, Kingsmill mentioning in particular Oriel House, which turned out to be the clergyman's own residence, and Pearson deploring that Minor Canon Row should have been defaced by the green railings. "It is the first time I've heard them complained of," said the clergyman. "But, perhaps . . . Now that (*pointing to a building in the Cathedral garden*) is an eyesore. It's the Choir School, and I should be very glad for the sake of the garden to see it taken down. But I fear it would be too costly."

"Surely," said Pearson, "it wouldn't cost much to have it removed?"

"Wouldn't the sale of the material, with everything so expensive nowadays, more than cover the cost of removing it?" asked Kingsmill.

"I'm afraid it's somewhat more complicated than that," said the clergyman, with a deprecating laugh. "You see, the Choir School would still have to be housed, and the rental would call for capital of from four to five thousand pounds. And," with a sigh, "I'm afraid we can't afford that."

He was so kindly, courteous and genial, and this picking about in the financial substructure of the church was so little in harmony with the ancient peace which enveloped them, that the travellers felt remorseful.

"Canon Crisparkle lived in this end house," said the clergyman. "*Edwin Drood*, you know. And John Jasper lived down there at the Gate House." The travellers did not kindle at this information; he seemed relieved at their apathy on the subject of Dickens, and telling them in answer to their enquiry that he was Dr. Mackean, Canon and Vice-Dean of the Cathedral, left with a friendly "Good-evening."

G. W. STONIER

While they were at work on the following Saturday, Pearson said that in looking for something he had come across a review of *This Blessed Plot* in which the critic had put them in the lowest grade of a class of writing represented at its best by Johnson and Boswell and in its middle state by Peacock or Belloc. "That no doubt expressed his real opinion," said Pearson. "But when he went on to compare us to a pantomime donkey, I felt that he was verging on the ungenerous."

KINGSMILL: There's always the risk, when reviewing a contemporary, that the final effect of the review may be encouraging. This is a risk against which G. W. Stonier, the writer of the review you mention, is usually careful to guard. I know him slightly, and he always reminds me of the Dormouse in *Alice*, I don't quite know why, except that the Dormouse is somewhat of an introvert. The writer he seems to like most is Joyce, and generally he's not ill-disposed towards anyone who prefers roaming through his own interior to mingling with other people. I like him and experience a faint glow when we meet, but he does nothing to fan it. A few months ago I came upon him in the London Library, asleep, with a book open on his knees. He looked discouraged and forlorn. I glanced at the book; it was entitled *La Mystère de Charité*, and I inferred from his baffled expression that the author had not proved helpful.

One day Pearson suggested to Kingsmill that they ought to balance Bernard Shaw with an equally illustrious veteran in the world of politics. "As a Worcester man, I've always felt, even if I have not always expressed, a warm feeling for Baldwin, which reached its zenith in April, 1932, when he made a speech at Stratford-on-Avon at the opening of the Shakespeare Memorial Theatre. He began with a sentence which, if other politicians took the same view, would get things into proper proportion and put politics where they belong—in the midden. Here it is: 'Such a gathering as this, an international gathering, would be impossible to celebrate the fame of any statesman, of any soldier, of any priest; and no money could buy it. It is only for a poet that such an assembly could be gathered together.' The man who can talk like that is worth seeing. What about it?"

KINGSMILL: Are we worth seeing by the man who can talk like that? I cannot at the moment recollect any particular reason why Baldwin should wish to see either of us, and I suspect that it would be useless to ransack my memory.

PEARSON: I'm Worcestershire on both sides, and Baldwin will know about my relatives, and may be willing to welcome us for their sake. But I shall, of course, explain that we are writing a book and wish to include in it a visit to him.

Having received a cordial invitation from Lord Baldwin, the travellers set out from Paddington for Worcester on Wednesday, May 22. It was the first really comfortable journey either of them had taken for some years; only one passenger in the first-class compartment, and he got out at

Oxford; and a delightful lunch by themselves in an airy, sunny section of the dining-car, from which they looked at the fields of buttercups and daisies and the glades and copses of the Western Midlands, more mysterious and richer but less radiant than the Southern country they knew so well.

They stayed at Ye Olde Talbot Inn, Kingsmill having liked the sound of it better than the Hop Market, which they later found to be the roomiest hotel in the town. "You may consider this place rather cramped," said Kingsmill as they unpacked in their double room, "but at any rate it's not The Old Talbot Inn, and I see from the lighting and general cleanliness that they renewed it from top to bottom before their consciences passed it as Ye Olde."

They crossed the street to a bookshop in a very old building, and as they sidled their way between piles of volumes and peered at crammed bookshelves, they felt again the excitement and mystery which bookshops had inspired in their youth, when dull books looked profound, and novels inlets into paradise, and dubious classics the repository of guilty felicities to be dreamed of but hardly to be attained. Pearson having bought *The Story of Francis Cludde* by Stanley Weyman and Kingsmill a volume of Lowell's *Essays*, they went on towards the Cathedral. In a bookshop opposite there was a placard bearing the words *Stamps for Sale*, and as Kingsmill had two unstamped postcards on him he went in and was informed, rather coldly, that the stamps in question were for collectors, not for correspondents. To retrieve the ground he had lost Kingsmill called to Pearson to join him, and they inspected the shelves.

PEARSON (*pointing to Algar Thorold's Life of Labouchere*):

I hope I didn't hasten Thorold's end, but I cannot claim to have delayed it. I'd just finished my own Life of Labby, and wrote to ask his permission to quote a few passages from his book. In giving it he said that he was very ill, and begged me not to quote his description of Labby's death, as its tone now distressed him, for he had become a Catholic. You remember the passage—''Flames? not yet, I think.'' But biographers have to sacrifice their and everyone else's private feelings, and I replied that I would take full responsibility after my own last words had been spoken for giving renewed currency to Labby's. Thorold died shortly afterwards, and whether this is the end of a short story or the middle of a serial remains to be seen.

Pearson having bought *Nero* by Stephen Phillips and Kingsmill a selection of Wordsworth's poems, they crossed over to the Cathedral. On the tower, outlined against the sky, stood a solitary figure whom Pearson surmised was Charles II, waiting until Cromwell had hacked his way through Friar Street before coming down and taking to his heels.

KINGSMILL: I must give the Stuarts the palm for cross-country running. There's Bonny Prince Charlie, my own favourite, loping across Scotland like a greyhound, from Inverness to Skye. There's Charles II doubling all over this part of England until he got into the straight on the South Downs.

PEARSON: And there's Charles I tacking from country house to country house, with Cromwell on his tail, and there's James II running, swimming, and certainly flying, with no one in pursuit.

As they came up to the Cathedral, Pearson commented on the reddish colouring of the stone, which, he said, was doubtless due to a strain in the neighbouring rock strata and went with the general rosiness of the town. They entered, and Pearson looking round said it gave him a strange feeling to realise how many of his kin, past and present, had preached within those walls. "It's a homely place," he went on; "very different from Winchester. None of those purse-proud prelates, but simple God-fearing men who have lived quietly down the ages on their three to five thousand a year."

They wandered round, noting with pleasure the scarcity of monuments and the unobtrusiveness of the choir screen. The only striking memorial was in the chancel, where the recumbent effigy of King John lay with its feet towards the altar. Pearson wondered whether, as most rulers had been so grossly overrated, John might not have suffered from the opposite process. "At least he loved Worcester, came here, I see, eight times and held his court here twice. A remarkable face—energy and self-pity in about equal proportions."

They had dinner at the Oyster Bar opposite the theatre. It was a roomy place, like an old-fashioned chop-house, and everything about it delighted them: the food was excellent, the diners few, and the waitresses really surprising after London in their anxiety to make them happy and satisfied. Dinner over, they walked down to the river; it was a warm evening, and they stood on the bridge. An engine outlined against the setting sun ran across the railway bridge upstream. Downstream the Cathedral on its high bank glowed in the evening light.

As they walked along the opposite bank they saw by the side of the path a white-haired woman lolling in the grass with a bottle of beer to her lips. Directly beyond her, on the other side of the river, stood a church with a high,

uncannily thin spire, bent at the top. Kingsmill said it had
the look of a building in a child's dream, and Pearson said
it was the object which, of all his early Worcester memories,
had stuck most clearly in his mind. As they went on, they
passed two care-free young soldiers arm in arm, who were
singing to the tune of "Red Sails in the Sunset":—

> Red stains on the carpet,
> Red stains on the knife,
> Oh Doctor Buck Ruxton,
> You murdered your wife.

The mist was rising in the fields, and on their way back,
passing the old woman, now fast asleep, they wondered
if they were justified in leaving her there. Would Dr.
Johnson? Pearson was inclined to think that Johnson
would have shouldered her and taken her home, but Kingsmill pointed out that the incident Pearson had in mind was
an isolated one, and that Johnson staggering along Fleet
Street with a woman on his back was not a nightly
spectacle. The woman in question had been turned out
into the street by her landlord and was crying for help.
The woman they had just passed had the air of one who
had sought the open of her own free will, and would not
be grateful to them if they dragged her back to harsh reality
from her present oblivion.

Passing up by the church with the high thin spire, they
found that its name was St. Andrews. It was shut up, and
had an air of long disuse and mouldering corruption.
"One doesn't want such a terrible witness as that to the
decay of Christianity," Pearson exclaimed, and starting
back a pace or two cried "There's a light inside! How
can there be? What does it mean?" However, it was not
the ghost of a past vicar mourning over the present

desolation, taper in hand, but a reflection from a neighbouring house caught by one of the few whole panes left
in the broken windows.

It was hot as a summer's day when they went out on the
following morning. Crossing the bridge again, they found
the old woman in the same place, peacefully asleep, her
face, ruddier than ever, turned up to the sun. A yard or two
away, propped on one elbow and looking glumly at the
river, reclined a man in his late thirties. It was clear that
he was on watch, and the travellers surmised that he was
the old woman's son-in-law, and had been sent there, in
accordance with the usual routine, to keep an eye on Ma
and bring her home if she would go with him quietly.
Looking back, from two or three hundred yards, they
saw the man rising and walking slowly and non-committally towards the bridge, as if ready instantly to retrace
his steps should Ma call or the Missus come in sight.

They sat basking in the sun on Severn bank for more
than an hour, and rose to return home as the Cathedral
chimes were playing "The Minstrel Boy."

EARL BALDWIN

Leaving Worcester after tea, Pearson and Kingsmill drove
along the Ombersley Road, which wound between
orchards and pasture land. They had been going for about
four miles when, pointing to a house some three hundred

yards from the road beyond a field of buttercups, Pearson said "That's Hawford, where I was born." In Ombersley itself he pointed to the church, where, he said, he was christened. A mile or two farther on they saw in the middle distance a white Georgian house on a slight eminence to which Pearson pointed, saying "That's Waresley Court, where my cousins the Gibbonses lived. One of them was my godfather. He gave me his name and left it at that." They passed through Stourport, and reached Astley Hall just before five. Lord Baldwin emerged from his study, leaning on a stick. "Come and see this before we talk," he said, and led them out on to the terrace behind the house, where, above two clipped yew trees, rose a mile or two away the tower of Astley Church and beyond it the Abberley Hills, clear against a rainy sky. Regretting that he could not take them to see a wider view, he told them he had arthritis, and there was nothing to be done about it—"One could keep three doctors going without doing oneself any good."

He showed them into his study, and took an armchair between them. Pearson, having learnt that the portrait over the mantelpiece was Lord Baldwin's father, asked if he too had lived at Astley Hall. No, said Lord Baldwin, he had himself bought Astley Hall forty years earlier. "My family came from Shropshire to make their money here, from Corvedale—a pretty title for my son" (with a smile). In reply to a question from Kingsmill, he said he did not care for *A Shropshire Lad* as much as he used to. He had met A. E. Housman at Cambridge, but the meeting had not been a very satisfactory one. "His poetry is easy to parody, and my friend G. M. Trevelyan has a collection of such parodies." Pearson said Kingsmill's was the best, and insisted that he should recite it. Lord Baldwin had already heard it from G. M. Trevelyan, so Kingsmill limited himself to one verse.

PEARSON: Did you know Elgar?

LORD BALDWIN: No, I'm sorry to say I didn't. As Prime Minister I was, I suppose, in a position to butt in on people, but I knew from my cousin Rudyard Kipling that writers and artists don't like being interrupted. I'm sorry to say I missed Thomas Hardy, too. No, I don't get much pleasure myself from his work, but he was a great writer, and I spoke about him in Dorchester early in this war. There were a thousand people present, and it was a little difficult in the open street, as you may imagine.

PEARSON: Do you read much nowadays? Kingsmill and I have just been re-reading Scott.

LORD BALDWIN: I'm delighted to hear you say that. I re-read the whole of Scott during the war. A great man as well as a great writer. I stayed at Melrose once, and had a whole day at Abbotsford to myself. Did you know that the original manuscript of Scott's *Journal* is now in America? It ought to be in Scotland. When I was settling the debt question over in the States, Pierpont Morgan was very kind to me. It was a wearying time, and I was glad to retreat to his library, and it was there that I found the manuscript of the *Journal*.

PEARSON: Was Kipling lovable?

LORD BALDWIN: *I* loved him. But it was difficult to get to know him. He didn't open out to many. With a pen in his hand he came to life, and would roar with laughter over his own things. He didn't mind me sitting there while he was working, and sometimes he would get up and walk up and down the garden chanting his poetry. It was only, he said, by singing it aloud that one could get poetry right.

PEARSON: Did you see much of him in London?

LORD BALDWIN: Occasionally at the Athenaeum. He said to me once that whenever he went into the lavatory there he expected to find a bishop on his back kicking his legs in the air like a black beetle. I was asked to write about him for the *Dictionary of National Biography*, and I had begun the article when my wife died. I had to give it up, but fortunately my good friend G. M. Young, who shares my dislike for the modern psychological approach in biographies, has taken it over. Kipling had the same dislike of connecting a man and his work. He wasn't given to personalities of any kind, and I never heard him express an opinion on any of his contemporaries, though there were two he mistrusted, not on literary grounds, but for their effect on the young.

PEARSON: Did you ever meet Bernard Shaw?

LORD BALDWIN: Yes. He came to see me once—it had to do with some matter relating to T. E. Lawrence. I had him in the Cabinet room at 10, Downing Street, and enjoyed his talk so much that I kept him for over an hour. He's extremely charming with one person, fidgety with two, and stands on his head with four.

KINGSMILL: Do you know H. G. Wells?

LORD BALDWIN: No, I have not met Wells.

KINGSMILL: Chesterton?

LORD BALDWIN: I am sorry to say no.

PEARSON: Didn't you really ever meet G. K. C.?

LORD BALDWIN: No, I never did. But I greatly admired his books on Dickens and Browning.

KINGSMILL: I remember Kipling in his autobiography

saying that Browning never took any notice of him when he was a child, and was, from the stand-point of a small boy, the least attractive of all the big persons who used to visit at his aunt's. Do you remember Browning too, and was that your impression of him?

LORD BALDWIN: No, I never saw Browning. But I must confess that, like William Morris, I've never paid much attention to children.

PEARSON: Good! Excellent!

LORD BALDWIN: I cling to my contemporaries. Did either of you know Q? There was a charming man. He understood how to make literature a living thing to the ordinary person. I am going to Cambridge soon. I'm always happy there. Everyone is very kind.

There was a pause, and Lord Baldwin said "Do you mind political gossip?" They were emphatic that they did not, and Lord Baldwin, after another pause, went on to characterise the oratory of some of his contemporaries.

LORD BALDWIN: Balfour used to snatch the words out of the air. Asquith produced words like bricks out of a box, and fitted them into a perfect pattern. He was the greatest of them all, a true classical orator.

KINGSMILL: What did you think of Lloyd George as a speaker?

LORD BALDWIN: Plenty of flame, though, unlike Asquith, he didn't read well, but I always enjoyed listening to the old ruffian—bless him! I remember at the time of the Maurice Debate meeting him in Whitehall. It was during the Coalition Government, and I was Financial Secretary to the Treasury. The Conservatives thought they'd got Lloyd George at last, and I said to him "My people have always been trying to catch you out in a lie, and they think they've

got you now. But all you have to do is to tell the truth."
He gave me a knowing smile and followed my advice.

KINGSMILL: He didn't manage the Marconi business so
adroitly.

LORD BALDWIN: It wasn't that he had done anything
wrong. If he had told the truth, everything would have been
quite simple. But he had been *silly*, and no one likes to
admit to that. He went about like a cornered rat those
days; his eyes were red and he snapped at everyone who
came near him. I remember him once saying to me "I've
been called a liar all my life, but then I've been out in
the rough and tumble. There's Bonar Law—he has a high
reputation for veracity. But what does he in his sheltered
life know of the kind of struggles I've been through?"

KINGSMILL: F. E. Smith was a fine speaker, wasn't he?
I was reading the other day about his brilliant replies in the
Lords when Carson was attacking him over the Irish
Settlement.

LORD BALDWIN: He was very clever indeed. Always
ready with a good thing. Once, when he was staying at
Wilton, Lord Pembroke was showing him the family
portraits, and told him that whenever one of his ancestors
had an illegitimate child he was given the name of Montgomery, to which F. E. Smith replied "If such an un-
toward event should happen to me, God forbid that I
should deny my child the name of Smith."

KINGSMILL: Did you know Beaverbrook?

LORD BALDWIN: Know Beaverbrook! I knew *him*. When
he first came over here, Kipling had great hopes of Beaverbrook. He'd just made a million in Canada, and wanted
to help the Empire, and that appealed to Kipling, who was
godfather to one of his sons. But Kipling quarrelled with

him over a change of policy in his papers. Kipling himself, as I daresay you know, threw up his job as leader-writer on an Indian paper because he refused to alter the editorial policy overnight. So the proprietor discharged him, and told him he would never earn more than three hundred a year.

PEARSON: You must have had a very trying time during the Abdication crisis.

LORD BALDWIN: It went off all right, but if it hadn't there would have been a bad mess.

PEARSON: Did you sleep well during it?

LORD BALDWIN: Yes, I never lost a night's sleep, and that was a great blessing. I'd been very ill before it, and I wondered if I would be able to see it through, but when it was over I never felt better in my life.

PEARSON: You did one of the most extraordinary things in history.

LORD BALDWIN: . . . It was a strange time.

After a brief pause, Lord Baldwin remarked that the two most difficult things he had handled were the Abdication and the General Strike. But of course neither of them was comparable to the situations which arose during a war. Kingsmill said he would have thought that it was much simpler to be Prime Minister during a war, when there was only one objective and everyone was agreed about tackling it.

PEARSON: In a war everybody is behind you. In peace large sections of the community are against you.

LORD BALDWIN: That is true, but the decisions a Prime Minister has to take in war are more terrible.

Pearson mentioning how delighted he had been by Lord Baldwin's speech on Shakespeare, and asking if it had been published in book form, Lord Baldwin rose and went to a bookshelf from which he took down *This Torch of Freedom*. "I am so glad you like that speech," he said. "I remember Bernard Shaw was in the audience, but he was not one of the speakers, and after I'd finished he said to a neighbour 'Thank God, the American Ambassador isn't speaking. We'd be here for another hour yet.'"

PEARSON: You must notice many changes in Worcestershire since your youth.

LORD BALDWIN: When I was a boy I could tell all the neighbours by the clop-clop of the horses' hoofs. But I was away for a generation, and when I returned everything was different.

PEARSON: Do you do much reading now?

LORD BALDWIN: A little light literature occasionally, but I spend most of my time meditating. I have a full head, and plenty to think about. I shall be seventy-nine in August and eighty in 1947. I am peeping over the edge, and feel like a disembodied spirit. (*To Pearson*) You are related to the Gibbonses, aren't you?

PEARSON: Yes, but how did you know it?

LORD BALDWIN: Ah, that is a fruit of my meditations.

Six o'clock struck, and the friends rose to go, but Lord Baldwin said they must stay and have a glass of perry. After a very enjoyable drink he took them through the dining-room and drawing-room. There were dust covers on the furniture, and in the drawing-room he said "This room will never be opened again."

Accompanying them into the drive he waved to them as they looked back on the way to their car. "Is that HIM?" the girl driver whispered. As they drove off, Pearson murmured "Very, very lovable," and Kingsmill gave an assenting nod.

Wandering through Worcester the following morning Pearson and Kingsmill admired the beautiful streets in which the new buildings harmonised so perfectly with the old red brick of the eighteenth century. Again they were struck by the courtesy of the inhabitants, which had been forcibly illustrated for them the previous evening by their driver. They had asked her, on reaching Worcester, how much they owed. ''I'm afraid it's a staggering price,'' she replied, stating after some hesitation that it would be 29s. 6d.–a sum by which they were indeed staggered, but in the other direction, since they had been driven nearly forty miles and had kept the car waiting for well over an hour.

Now, on going into a tobacconist, they were thanked for buying a box of matches and a packet of pipe-cleaners, neither of which, they agreed, could have been obtained in London except as a sequel to a purchase of tobacco, and then only under unspoken protest and sullen resistance to an unreasonable and capricious request.

They had a farewell lunch at the Oyster Bar, and as they were leaving told the lady at the desk how much they had appreciated the food and the service. Her husband was Swiss, she said, and that was why the service was so good; his name was Perrenoud and he came from Neuchâtel. Kingsmill, when they were outside, was disposed on the score of this information to deduct a little from the swelling account of Pearson's native city, but Pearson was quite agreeable to Switzerland gaining what Worcester lost in view of the fact that one of his sixteen great-great-grandparents was, like Monsieur Perrenoud, a native of French Switzerland.

PEARSON IN ACTION

After their day's work on Saturday, June 1, they went as usual to the Cosmo in Finchley Road, an excellent restaurant where they were able, in the company of the natives of those parts, to enjoy sauerkraut with their boiled beef. On returning to Pearson's house they discovered that the catch had slipped and let down the Yale lock in the front door. Pearson's latch key was therefore of no use, and as the windows were all bolted and neither of the travellers could see his way to adopting Mrs. Pearson's suggestion that one of them should swarm up a drain-pipe and squeeze through the lavatory window, they borrowed a knife from a next-door neighbour, and Kingsmill watched Pearson working it to and fro between the sashes of the basement window without effect except on his temper. A neighbouring clock had long struck ten, and Pearson and Kingsmill were standing listlessly outside the front door, speaking at random of locksmiths, policemen, ladders and friends they had known who were good with their hands. "In the last emergency," said Pearson, "I shall be compelled to drive the door in by main force."

"How?" asked Kingsmill.

"Like this," said Pearson. "I insert my latchkey—so—turn it—so—and then . . ." He raised his foot, and brought the flat of his shoe smartly against the door, which opened and they went in.

One day Pearson proposed to Kingsmill that they should go to Chigwell to have a look at the King's Head, the original of the Maypole in *Barnaby Rudge*.

PEARSON: I was re-reading *Barnaby Rudge* recently, and discovered that Dickens, who was the first writer to deify the common man, was also the only writer to divine what would happen when the common man became *deus*. His Simon Tappertit in *Barnaby Rudge* is Charlie Chaplin playing the part of Adolf Hitler, each of whom typifies the common man, one in art, the other in action. You yourself in *The Poisoned Crown* have noticed the odd resemblance between these two, but Dickens noticed it long before they were born. Tappertit, you may remember, is a little man in every sense. His mind is as small as his body, which is about a couple of jampots high. He has a searching look, hypnotic eyes that pierce like gimlets, a naturally shrill voice which takes on a hoarse note if necessary, and a theatrical manner. When moody he marches about with his arms folded, and on account of his greatness he can only afford to be merry now and then. He is the chief of a secret society of Prentice Knights, who plot revenge against their masters and arrange to beat up everyone who gets on their nerves. When Tappertit learns that the girl he wishes to marry loves another, he says to himself "Very good. His days are numbered," and promptly opens a campaign to number them. The fulsome praise of his satellites drives him on; a voice within him keeps whispering "Greatness"; and he feels his soul getting into his head at the idea. He calls himself the healer of the

wounds of his unhappy country, and at the crucial moment
of action cries "My bleeding country calls me and I go!"
Foreshadowing the Nazis' Munich cellar, Dickens shows
Tappertit and his fellow-gangsters meeting in a dungeon,
where the Fuehrer, with a thigh-bone for sceptre, dispenses
judgment from a chair of state which is mounted on a
large table ornamented with a brace of skulls. Such is the
will-power in Dickens himself that he could extract out of
his own interior the synthetic forms the two great Common
Men of our time would take, Chaplin, whose personality
was built up by the film, Hitler, whose personality was
built up by the wireless; Tappertit being a sort of auto-
maton who moves with the jerky unreality of the silent
picture and speaks with the metallic unreality of the radio
voice. But the most amazing thing of all is that Dickens
instinctively felt the very sound of the names by which the
little man would achieve his apotheosis—Tappertit containing TAP for CHAP, and TIT for HIT, and ER for ER.

CHIGWELL

Emerging from Chigwell station on the afternoon of
June 5, they walked up the hill and came to the King's
Head, a delightful inn opposite a cosy old church set in
bright meadowland and spinneys.

KINGSMILL: Well, not much of this sunlight got into
Dickens's Chigwell. His Maypole is a mixture of fantasy
and gloom, environed with twilit woods and approached

through darkling lanes. I daresay that in the original draft of *Barnaby Rudge* there was a monkey called Gobbels, ceaselessly chattering as he swung by his tail from one of the rafters.

The King's Head was closed on the street side, so they went round to the back, and found an old gardener who said that if they wanted tea they would have to go on to Abridge. "How far is Heybridge?" asked Kingsmill. "It's only a few minutes to Abridge on the bus," the gardener replied. They went back to the road, and as the bus came along Kingsmill exclaimed "But it *is* Abridge, after all." "After all what?" asked Pearson. "After all my inability to grasp that the gardener had his aspirates in perfect control."

In Abridge they had tea in a canteen behind a shop called Brighty's, and afterwards sat on the wall at the end of the yard, beneath them a swiftly flowing stream over which the swallows were darting, and beyond the stream rich meadow-land which stretched to a low line of tree-covered hills.

In the evening, after supper at the Café Royal, they walked down to the Club through St. James's Park, where the illuminations for Victory Day were being rehearsed. There were few people about, and they had an undisturbed view of the many-coloured fountains splashing in the lake, somewhat to the surprise, it seemed, of the ducks who were paddling about uncertainly, as if fearful of leaving a blue stretch of water for an orange, or a yellow for a red.

A bold tactical stroke, the taking of a 31 bus from Swiss Cottage to Chelsea, enabled the travellers to dispose of the most significant portions of residential London in one movement. Having examined the meteorological situation in the morning papers of Wednesday, June 12, they started off at eleven-thirty.

PEARSON: Hampstead apart, St. John's Wood is beyond all cavil or question the most delightful residential quarter of London—the exquisite Regency houses, the gardens and the tree-lined roads, the close proximity of Primrose Hill and Regent's Park, the brisk but not too piercing air peculiar to the lower slopes of mountains—it is these that drew me here and have kept me here, though whether St. John's Wood plus Pearson outweighs Hampstead minus, it is not for me to say.

While the bus traversed the squalid district between Kilburn High Road and Westbourne Grove, Kingsmill mused on the case for Bayswater.

KINGSMILL: Bayswater, so far as I remember it before 1914, was still the prosperous district which provoked the scorn of the late Victorian aesthetes because it was respectable, and the contempt of Kensington because it was middle-class. I remember an old lady telling me that when she was young she and her sister, who were living in Kensington, used to madden an aunt by putting Bayswater on their letters to her; but the Bayswater I have lived in off and on since 1927, and have a real affection for, is the easy-going Bayswater of hotels and boarding-houses, competently and conscientiously run by the class of woman who used to live in Kensington.

PEARSON: Look at those wooden stakes round that garden! The one great benefit of the war was the removal of railings from parks and squares. True, it was a bit excessive to convert Europe and Asia into a blood-bath merely in order to get rid of our park palings, but I would favour a second and local blood-bath to prevent their restoration.

KINGSMILL: There's Campden Hill, and having spent more than half of the war in Holland Park, I too can claim whatever benefits attach to the brisk air of the lower slopes. I love Holland Park, but I don't care for Kensington. It's neither hill nor river, but as it were an after-dinner sleep, dreaming of neither.

PEARSON: Just the kind of indeterminate place dear old Thackeray would live in, but he gives it a sort of sleepy charm in *Esmond* where he describes the town house of Lord Castlewood.

Thackeray's House, Young Street, Kensington

THE PRAM AND THE SCREEN

They had left the High Street behind them when suddenly Kingsmill exclaimed "Good God! Lexham Gardens! Let's get off at once. Harris! you remember." Pearson tumbled down the bus stairs in Kingsmill's wake, and they paused to collect themselves on the pavement.

KINGSMILL: It was 67, wasn't it, where Frankie lived?

PEARSON: It most emphatically was. And it's thirty-three years almost to the month since I was last there.

KINGSMILL: And it's just over thirty-three years since I would have been repulsed from the door if I had been so ill-advised as to ring the bell. I joined Frankie's Iscariots in the February of 1913.

PEARSON: And I was being groomed for the Beloved Disciple round about June, but as I was on the stage I didn't see enough of him to get into the Iscariot class by 1914, when as you know he went to quod and then to France before his creditors could nab him.

KINGSMILL: Well, here it is. I remember one evening, when we had come back from a walk, he paused on those steps and said "It's a very good thing for both of us that we met." I must admit to a faint feeling of remorse whenever I recall this remark, made as it was in the hope that the Gospel according to St. Hugh would preserve in its pristine freshness the image of the Master impressed upon my mind during our many evening rambles.

They entered the hall of 67 and stood at the door of the ground floor flat.

KINGSMILL: I wish we could have a look inside, but I don't see a bell, and in any case the place seems deserted.

They drifted out to the porch, and Kingsmill, feeling

that it was useless to press the bell marked 67 but anxious to press a bell of some kind, pressed 67a, above which was a plate with the name of Rawlinson, and hastened into the street to await developments.

KINGSMILL: Thank goodness, no one's coming. I haven't the slightest idea what we can say if anyone does.

PEARSON: You mean, what *you* can say. I leave the matter entirely in your hands.

As he spoke, Pearson saw a tall military figure descending the hall stairs, with the stern deliberation of one who, while not prejudging the situation, would not be satisfied unless it was made perfectly clear to him why he had been brought down. "This must be Rawlinson," said Pearson. "I'm going." "Just one moment," said Kingsmill.

"Yes?" enquired the figure, appearing in the doorway.

KINGSMILL: Oh—sorry—but we wondered if we could have a look at the downstairs flat. The fact is, we used to know someone who lived there.

MR. RAWLINSON: Yes?

KINGSMILL: I must have pressed the wrong bell.

MR. RAWLINSON: Yes.

KINGSMILL: It's a long time ago. Thirty-three years. Our friend's name was Frank Harris.

MR. RAWLINSON: I knew Frank Harris.

PEARSON: Good God!

KINGSMILL: Did you really? Of course, he was an old rascal, and it must seem odd our coming on a pilgrimage to his flat. But we both had a high opinion of him when we were young.

MR. RAWLINSON: I've lived here since 1909, and I remember him well. And his wife too—a very decorative woman.

PEARSON: How extraordinary that you were up there when we were down here thirty-three years ago! It's . . . it's incredible. Did you run into them at all?

MR. RAWLINSON: My wife and I didn't know them personally. But they had a lot of visitors, and didn't like the baby's pram standing in the hall. So when they gave parties they used to ask us if we would take the pram up to our flat. We didn't object to that, but Harris used also to place a screen at the bottom of our stairs. Of course I always removed it. I used to put it up against this wall.

Mr. Rawlinson, they learnt, had retired from the Phoenix Insurance, but still edited their paper. During the war he had been a Commandant in the Special Constabulary, a post he still held.

PEARSON: Would you support a proposal to put a plaque up here in memory of Harris?

MR. RAWLINSON: Why not? With Ichabod on it. They arrested him here and he was marched off between two policemen.

Promising Mr. Rawlinson to send him their book, they went on their way.

PEARSON: Frankie wouldn't have got much change out of Rawlinson. He's the type that Frankie really respected, though he preferred to write about Shakespeare, Christ and Oscar Wilde. I'll bet he never replaced the screen after Rawlinson had put it against the wall.

KINGSMILL: How like Frankie to put up that screen! He must have been under the impression that for some occult reason the veiling of the stairs would delude his visitors into supposing that the whole house was his. I can't remember ever noticing the stairs, though I presume they weren't curtained off on my behalf, but it never occurred to me that Frankie was occupying the whole house, and if it didn't occur to me it certainly wouldn't have occurred to the older and wealthier visitors, who stood to lose if they made mistakes about his financial position.

96, Cheyne Walk, (Whistler, 1866–78)

TAM

Resuming their southerly journey on a 31 bus, they got out at World's End and walked down to Chelsea Embankment.

PEARSON: This Embankment has some charming houses, but I've never liked Chelsea, in spite of the fact that Tam and Oscar lived here. It's a little unreal, like the people, unfortunately including Oscar and Tam, who have inhabited it. Rossetti's unreal, Whistler's unreal, Henry James is unreal, Sir Thomas More was a lawyer, an M.P., a Catholic saint and the first Utopian, and, to pass from the unreal to the fantastic, we have Swinburne, Meredith and Hall Caine. But here we are at Cheyne Row, so let's call on Tam.

They entered Carlyle's house, now 24 Cheyne Row, and were shown over the rooms by the guardian, Mrs. Strong. Kingsmill, moved by the tortured expression in a portrait of Jane Carlyle, expressed himself emphatically to Pearson about the horror of being cooped up with Tam, but was sternly taken to task by Mrs. Strong, who quoted many favourable verdicts on Carlyle passed by people who did not have to live with him. Kingsmill withstood the assault for a time, but presently thought it expedient to shorten his line, withdraw to prepared positions in the rear, vacate them as the enemy advanced, and finally leave the field.

Jane's four-poster bed in her room on the first floor seemed to the visitors to be still penetrated by the intense melancholia of its years-long solitary occupant, and they thought of her nerves jangling hour after hour as her husband paced his room above, agog for any cockcrow which might pierce the sound-proof walls.

24, Cheyne Row

The late bombing, they were interested to learn, had spared everything in the house except the death mask of Cromwell, which it had split, and the plaster in the sound-proof room where *Frederick the Great* was written. However, the damage to Cromwell had been put right, and Frederick's cunning, mean and callous face still disfigured the staircase wall.

As they came down from the top floor Pearson said that after all the Tam they cherished must not be confused with the poor demented creature who wasted the better part of his working life celebrating Cromwell for all the wrong things and concocting right things in Frederick to celebrate. Kingsmill had recently passed on to Pearson a story he had heard from E. S. P. Haynes. Joseph Chamberlain, at the height of his fame as a Radical politician, visited Carlyle one day with W. H. Mallock, who had just come down from Oxford with the reputation of a brilliant youth with a great career before him. Mallock, apparently, had been too brilliant during the visit, for, as he and Chamberlain were putting their coats on, Carlyle, who had gone up the first flight of stairs, leant over the balustrade and called out "Can ye hear me, Mr. Mallock?" Mallock having expectantly signified that he could, and no doubt thrown himself into a cordially receptive posture, Carlyle continued: "I didna enjoy your veesit, and I dinna want to see ye again."

PEARSON: It must have been over this very balustrade Carlyle leaned. One can assume that Mallock had no premonition of the impending avalanche, and beamed upwards at the sage; but what would Chamberlain look like while waiting for Carlyle's parting word? He'd want to take due credit for introducing this young wonder, if credit was coming, but was it? He'd be keeping his line of retreat open. So his expression must have mingled a readiness to endorse Carlyle's approval with an equal readiness to jettison Mallock, should jettisoning be the order of the day.

They went out into the street and Pearson paused. "It

was on this spot, and not a foot farther, that Mallock got his congé. 'Well, Mr. Mallock, that's your way. This is mine. Good day.' ''

HILAIRE BELLOC

One day in Pearson's flat, taking Belloc from the shelves, Kingsmill remarked ''I don't quite know what Belloc's a Grand Old Man of, but he's clearly a Grand Old Man of something—seafaring, perhaps, or tramping or anti-Free-masonry or pro-Semitism or distributing other people's property or enlarging his own or Catholicism or Paganism.''

PEARSON: The trouble with Belloc is that he has dissipated his genius, of which I've always felt he had a larger share than any of his contemporaries. Had he stuck to the kind of thing he did in *The Path to Rome*, he'd have produced a little library of outdoor and indoor scenes, scraps of poetry, humorous dialogues and miscellaneous reflections, which would have given Bellocianism as great a significance in literature as Rabelaisianism has now.

KINGSMILL (*opening The Path to Rome*): This is a really wonderful passage, thoughts at evening in an Italian village, the best and deepest thing he ever wrote: ''In very early youth the soul can still remember its immortal habitation, and clouds and the edges of hills are of another kind from ours, and every scent and colour has a savour of Paradise. What that quality may be no language can tell, nor have men made any words, no, nor any music, to recall it—only in a transient way and elusive the recollection of what youth was, and purity, flashes on us in the phrases of the poets, and is gone before we can fix it in our minds. Whatever those sounds may be that are beyond our sounds, whatever is Youth—youth came up that valley at evening, borne upon a southern air. If we desire or attain beatitude, such things shall at last be our settled state; and their now sudden influence upon the soul in short ecstasies is the proof that they stand outside time, and are not subject to decay.''

PEARSON: Yes, that's the top note of the book, but there's another passage which moves me equally, because it's a picture of the solitude from which he was sometimes able to escape in his youth but which even then was always closing round him again. Here it is: ''They drank my wine, I ate their bread, and we parted: they to go to their accustomed place, and I to cross this unknown valley. But when I had left these grave and kindly men, the echo of their voices remained with me; the deep valley of the Enza seemed lonely, and as I went lower and lower down towards the noise of the river I lost the sun.''

The friends having agreed that a visit to Belloc would be well worth making, Kingsmill, on the advice of his brother Arnold Lunn, wrote to Hilaire Belloc's daughter, Mrs. Jebb, asking if he and his friend might come down to see her father, and mentioning that they were writing a book which would include an account of their visit. Mrs. Jebb sent them a very friendly reply, and on Wednesday, June 19, they set out for Horsham.

''By the way,'' Kingsmill remarked to Pearson as the train approached Horsham, ''we can't have all the most illustrious men in England waving regretful farewells to us. Our readers may be able to stand the twilight valedictions of Shaw and Baldwin, but if Belloc also semaphores through the dusk there will be trouble."

"There's not the slightest risk of that, not even if we stand there flapping at him for half-an-hour."

After a very pleasant lunch at the King's Head, Horsham, a stroll round the old town by Pearson and a nap by Kingsmill, and a pleasant tea by both, they took the Worthing bus, which dropped them about two miles from King's Land, Hilaire Belloc's house. On their way towards it the long ridge of the South Downs came into view, and Pearson said "Well, he's ending in the place he cared for most and has written his best verses on—

> I never get between the pines
> But I smell the Sussex air,
> Nor I never come on a belt of sand
> But my home is there;
> And along the sky the line of the Downs
> So noble and so bare."

King's Land stood just off a lane, a comfortable old farm-house which seemed a part of the fields and trees around it. From the garden path they stepped straight into a large living-room through a door set in a wide window, and were cordially welcomed by Mr. and Mrs. Jebb, with whom they talked for a few minutes. "We will leave you now," murmured Mrs. Jebb, as her father came in.

Kingsmill having been introduced to Hilaire Belloc as Arnold Lunn's brother, Belloc shook Pearson's hand and asked after Arnold Lunn. He had grown a beard since they had last seen him, and his expression was more sombre, though he seemed in good health. They seated themselves, and Pearson applied a match to Belloc's pipe.

HILAIRE BELLOC: Any news from town?

PEARSON: Of what kind?

HILAIRE BELLOC: Political. I get all my news from private people. The papers put in what they know, but they know nothing.

The visitors having indicated that they were in the same position as the papers, Kingsmill led the talk to Oxford, mentioning R. S. Rait and Herbert Fisher, both of whom had been Fellows at New College in his time as well as in Belloc's.

HILAIRE BELLOC: Fisher wanted to get me a Fellowship at New College. And Trinity wanted me, too, but the dons were frightened. They didn't know what I'd do. I might come into the Common Room with a girl over my shoulder.

KINGSMILL: Why didn't they give you a Fellowship at Balliol, your own College?

HILAIRE BELLOC: Oh, no. That was out of the question. Jowett looked on Catholics as a sect. I would have liked a Fellowship, and if they'd given me a lot of money, I'd have taken one. I was married and they weren't paying enough.

PEARSON: Who was the "remote and ineffectual don who dared attack your Chesterton"?

HILAIRE BELLOC: No one in particular. Any don.

KINGSMILL: You were up with F. E. Smith, weren't you? What did you think of him?

HILAIRE BELLOC: Superficial. No brains. A politician.

KINGSMILL: John Simon?

HILAIRE BELLOC: Much better brains than Smith. Smith wanted to be President of the Union in the summer. That's the important term for the people who want to get on. He came to me and begged me to take the Presidency in the Easter term. I didn't mind. I let him have what he wanted.

Pearson: Did you know Winston Churchill?

Hilaire Belloc: Intimately. A genial fellow. A Yankee, of course. His mother was a Jerome.

Kingsmill: I suppose you knew Lloyd George, too?

Hilaire Belloc: Intimately. A little country solicitor who got on. Made a lot of money but didn't know how.

Pearson: How did Asquith strike you?

Hilaire Belloc: Good, straightforward brain. Knew nothing about France. No English politician does. The Irish were the only good speakers in Parliament. Parnell was ruined by the Irish Catholics. Catholicism is very Puritan in Ireland.

Pearson: You knew Labouchere?

Hilaire Belloc: Intimately.

Pearson: He wasn't the ordinary politician.

Hilaire Belloc: He spoke the truth about everything except the Foreign Office. He'd been one of them.

Kingsmill: I suppose you were in time to hear Gladstone speak.

Hilaire Belloc: He knew nothing. Talked nonsense in a magnificent way. The official style of the period.

Kingsmill: Did you ever meet Kipling?

Hilaire Belloc: Never. He wrote trash. But my mother had a high opinion of Soldiers Three, and she was a good judge.

Kingsmill: He loved France.

Hilaire Belloc: Knew nothing about it. The ordinary English gentleman knows nothing about it, but Kipling knew less than nothing.

Kingsmill: Have you a nostalgia for France?

Hilaire Belloc: Why?

Kingsmill: Aren't there any parts of it you'd like to see again? The Loire, or Normandy?

HILAIRE BELLOC: I know the whole of France. But I know Alsace best. That was where I did my service. Knew every inch of the ground.

PEARSON: How long were you in the French army?

HILAIRE BELLOC: A year—and a little.

PEARSON: How did you manage to get out of it so soon?

HILAIRE BELLOC: I pulled strings. I'd a cousin in the French Government.

PEARSON: You would know a great deal about French politics from the inside?

HILAIRE BELLOC: It was the Dreyfus case that opened my eyes to the Jew question. I'm not an anti-Semite. I love 'em, poor dears. Get on very well with them. My best secretary was a Jewess. Poor darlings—it must be terrible to be born with the knowledge that you belong to the enemies of the human race.

KINGSMILL: Why do you say the Jews are the enemies of the human race?

HILAIRE BELLOC: The Crucifixion.

KINGSMILL: I see.

PEARSON: You must have influenced G. K. C. a lot?

HILAIRE BELLOC: People said Chesterton took all his ideas from my talk. It's not true, not true at all. It was from my books he took them, whole passages, perhaps without knowing it. He popularised my ideas on property—for the middle classes. He was a poor speaker. His brother Cecil was a better speaker and a better writer. A very able man.

PEARSON: Do you like Shaw?

HILAIRE BELLOC: One of the kindest men alive. A tolerable speaker—Irish verve. Very generous to all kinds of

persons one knows nothing about. By the way, is it true
that H. G. Wells is eighty years old? I can't believe it.

KINGSMILL: Yes, he was born in '66.

HILAIRE BELLOC: I'm seventy-six. Shan't be eighty for
another four years.

PEARSON: Are you going to give us an autobiography?

HILAIRE BELLOC: No. No gentleman writes about his
private life. Anyway, I hate writing. I wouldn't have
written a word if I could have helped it. I only wrote for
money. *The Path to Rome* is the only book I ever wrote for
love.

PEARSON: Didn't you write *The Four Men* for love?

HILAIRE BELLOC: No. Money.

PEARSON: *The Cruise of the Nona?*

HILAIRE BELLOC: Money.

KINGSMILL: That's a wonderful passage in *The Path to
Rome*, about youth borne up the valley on the evening
air.

HILAIRE BELLOC: Oh—yes.

KINGSMILL: I love the poetry in your essays, especially in
the volume *On Nothing.*

HILAIRE BELLOC: Quite amusing. Written for money.

PEARSON: What profession would you have liked to
follow?

HILAIRE BELLOC: I was called to the Bar. But what I
wanted to be was a private gentleman. Lazing about doing
nothing. Farm as a hobby, perhaps. Keep someone to run it.

PEARSON: Have you read your sister's delightful memoirs?

HILAIRE BELLOC: I hear they're very good. Never read
them myself. Perhaps I might write my impressions of
some contemporaries, but I don't like even that.

KINGSMILL: Mrs. Belloc Lowndes has a charming account

of her friendship with Verlaine. What do you think of his poetry?

HILAIRE BELLOC: My French vocabulary is limited. I can't tell good verse from bad. I've always liked Paul Déroulède's work, but my French friends tell me it's not poetry.

Mr. and Mrs. Jebb returned, and the visitors rose to take their leave. Pearson had just asked Belloc what he thought of Stalin, and as they shook hands Belloc said "Very mediocre intelligence. Don't know why he's where he is. Remember me to your brother."

Mr. and Mrs. Jebb walked with them down the road and saw them into the car which had come to pick them up. In the evening light the South Downs were clearly defined against the sky, and they remembered the verse which follows Belloc's praise of their bare and noble line—

> A lost thing could I never find,
> Nor a broken thing mend;
> And I fear I shall be all alone
> When I get towards the end.
> Who will there be to comfort me,
> Or who will be my friend?

SOLUTION BY TAXI

There being still portions of the Metropolis unvisited by the travellers, they determined to cover them by car, and on Thursday afternoon, June 27, left the Club in a taxi, their first halt being St. Bartholomew, the oldest parish church in London.

North Ambulatory, St. Bartholomew's the Great

KINGSMILL: I was here once or twice when my son Brooke was in the choir; and the rector told me that the church was badly in need of funds.

PEARSON: Well, if there's a single church in London that ought to be preserved in its ancient glory, this is it. Here goes half-a-crown, anyway. Durham Cathedral apart, this is the finest example of Norman architecture I know. Solidified history. One really gets the feeling, looking through those arches at the sky, that the England of eight hundred years ago is lying outside there, Chaucer and Shakespeare and everyone still to come.

KINGSMILL: I see from this leaflet that it was founded by Henry I's Jester, Rahere. Rather an elaborate joke perhaps, but, of course, the Jester of those times had to play many parts—sage, minstrel, chronicler and all the other things which would fall to the lot of the only man at court who could spell—a sort of Beachcomber, Arthur Bryant, Noel Coward, Hansard, Whitaker's Almanac, Bradshaw and Black Marketeer rolled into one. This church doubtless represents conscience money, and as there is still plenty of occasion for conscience money I hope some of it will come this way to keep the church in repair.

PEARSON: It's strange to think that everyone of note since Henry I has been within these walls, has passed or looked at that very pillar, which was standing there while the poor wretches just outside in Smithfield were being roasted at the stake by our Winchester friend Stephen Gardiner.

From St. Bartholomew they drove to Holborn Viaduct Station, which they found had been badly bombed, the western side of the station and nearly the whole of the hotel having gone. They wanted to see the place where Samuel Butler and Festing Jones had stood, the tears trickling down their beards, as the train bore their young Swiss friend, Hans Faesch, out into the raw and windy night. Jones had made Hans's acquaintance eighteen months earlier in the train between Basle and Calais, and he and Butler had lavished affection and attention on the young man throughout his stay in England. Butler's anguish at the parting was expressed in some verses:

> The wind is heavy with snow and the sea rough,
> He has a racking cough and his lungs are weak.
> Hand in hand we watch the train as it glides
> Out, out, out into the night.
> So take him into thy holy keeping, O Lord,
> And guide him and guard him ever, and fare him well!

It was on February 14, 1895, that Hans left from Holborn Viaduct. On the same evening a fashionable audience was gathering at the St. James's Theatre for the first performance of *The Importance of Being Earnest*, and the Marquis of Queensberry was assembling his nosegay of root vegetables which he intended to fling at Oscar Wilde when he took his curtain at the end of the play.

KINGSMILL: I've never seen such a low roof in a station, so cramping, so clamping down. Even with the light let in by the bombs at that end, this station still symbolises Victorian oppression more completely than any other. Poor old Sam—it was a perfect setting for his open-as-the-day feeling for that brisk young commercial traveller, towards whom, as he explained with such care, he felt all that can legitimately be felt by one man for another. I don't know whether it's more pathetic or comic, the thought of those two whiskered and weeping Platonists in those curious late Victorian hats which combined the dignity of a topper and the sturdiness of a bowler.

PEARSON: I'd feel more sympathy for them if they'd felt more sympathy for Wilde. But after his condemnation, Sam funked publishing the Ode to Faesch. He thought it might be open to misconstruction. In other words, he knew that only one construction could be put upon it. That was bad enough, but after Wilde had gone to prison Butler and Jones concocted a private little joke of their own. Whenever either of them caught a bug in his bed, apparently a fairly frequent occurrence, he would speak of it as an "Osc."

At this point, Pearson beginning in swelling tones to institute a comparison between the private lives of Wilde and Butler, Kingsmill hurried him into the station bar, where, after a double whisky, he returned to the historic memories of the place. "It was," he said, "on one of the now vanished upper floors of this building that Wilde lunched with Robert Ross and Alfred Douglas after the collapse of his case against Queensberry and a few hours before his arrest. I don't know whether he had a racking cough or what his lungs were like, but I personally find this scene more moving than the departure of a brisk young commercial traveller on his lawful occasions."

On getting out at St. Paul's Cathedral, Pearson remarked reassuringly to the driver "We won't be so long as the size of this building might lead you to expect." They entered and walked rapidly up the north aisle.

PEARSON: St. Paul's is the most wonderful building in the world. It symbolises the English people, their capital, their country and their Empire.

KINGSMILL: But, like most things, it's better seen at a distance. From Hampstead Heath it's poetry; here it's rather heavy prose, except for this magnificent dome which is epic not lyrical. As for these unspeakable statues. . . . Look at that one of your hero Sir Henry Lawrence. It might have been done by a gifted inmate of a home for imbeciles trying to imitate Rodin's Shaw.

As they turned towards the south aisle, they half glanced at a huge figure of J. M. W. Turner, and quickened their steps. "Everything's here," muttered Pearson. "The vulgarity as well as the magnificence of empire." Once more in their taxi, Kingsmill asked Pearson if he had noticed the Turner statue, and, on Pearson nodding, said "I didn't want to mention it to you, but when I saw you didn't want to mention it to me, I had to mention it to you." Pearson nodded again. "Anyway," continued Kingsmill, "those statues don't matter five minutes after seeing them. Only the building matters. After Churchill the man of the last war to whom I personally am most grateful is Ronald James Smith, of Edgware, Middlesex, who was awarded the G.M., and ought to have been given a million pounds with it, for saving St. Paul's from destruction by an unexploded mine. He'd just begun to put the mine out

The George Inn, Southwark

of action when the vibration of a passing fire-engine started the clockwork of the fuse, and he got in the safety gag with only a second or two to spare. If St. Paul's had gone, half the morale of London would have gone with it. As long as it was there, there didn't seem much to worry about.''

The taxi drew up outside Southwark Cathedral.

PEARSON: The only thing to remember here is that Shakespeare's feet pressed these stones, under penalty of a severe fine if they didn't. Driver, the Club.

On their way back, approaching St. Paul's from the east, they were enraptured by the vast expanse which the bombs had cleared. "This," said Pearson, "is far and away the finest near view of St. Paul's. All these bombed spaces should be turned into gardens and preserved as a permanent

219

Dr. Johnson's House, Gough Square

memorial to the dead and a permanent refreshment for the living." Stopping the taxi half-way up Fleet Street, and turning into Gough Square, they paused opposite Johnson's house. Kingsmill said he had often come that way from *Punch* during the war. In the blackout the building had been clearly outlined against the night sky, and it was easy to imagine Johnson in one of the upper rooms writing *Rasselas* to pay for his mother's funeral, and reconciled with life, which had been so painful to him, as he looked back upon it through the eyes of Imlac, the sage: "My retrospect of life recalls to my view many opportunities of good neglected, much time squandered upon trifles, and more lost in idleness and vacancy. I leave many great designs unattempted, and many great attempts unfinished. My mind is burdened with no heavy crime, and therefore I compose myself to tranquillity; endeavour to abstract my thoughts from hopes and cares which, though reason knows them to be vain, still try to keep their old possession of the heart; expect, with serene humility, that hour which nature cannot long delay, and hope to possess in a better state that happiness which here I could not find, and that virtue which here I have not attained.''

THE CLIFFORD BAX SHAKESPEARE

Kingsmill, who had already seen Clifford Bax's portrait of Shakespeare three times since its purchase by Bax early in 1945, had long wanted Pearson to see it too. A reproduction of it in a Sunday paper had disinclined Pearson to view the original; but he yielded at last, and at six on Monday, July 1, accompanied by John Trevor, who had just returned from a successful tour of the Middle East, they called on Clifford Bax in the Albany. Their host, who was suffering from gout, welcomed them with the old-world courtesy peculiar to that complaint; and while John Trevor deftly and gracefully attended to the drinks, Clifford Bax told Pearson about the portrait. This, he said, was the story. After the 1715 rising Lord Nithsdale escaped from the Tower and fled to Rome. The household effects of the Jacobite refugees on the Continent were often brought over from England by their relatives, and this painting was taken out to Lord Nithsdale by his wife, and left to a monastery on his death, with a statement that it was a portrait of Shakespeare. There it had remained for some two hundred years; shortly before the war a priest had brought it to England and had been interned in the Isle of Man before he could dispose of it. On his release, Bax, by some strange chance, stranger perhaps because he had himself written a play on Lord Nithsdale, met him and was told of the portrait. He saw it, felt at once that it was genuine, and became its owner. "There it is," he concluded, waving his hand towards it.

To Kingsmill's satisfaction, Pearson at once accepted it as the authentic head and countenance of Shakespeare.

PEARSON: From the reproduction it struck me as an entirely miserable face, but here, thank God, is humour.

CLIFFORD BAX: That's quick of you. It took me some time to discover the humour.

PEARSON: The man who once wrote Falstaff is lurking behind the man who has just written *Timon*. It shows great suffering.

KINGSMILL: A generous mouth distorted by bitterness and frustration.

CLIFFORD BAX: It is a snarling nose. An expert whom I invited to examine the portrait assured me that there were only two genuine likenesses of Shakespeare in existence, the Droeshout and the Stratford bust, and that therefore this could not be genuine. I confess the logic of this argument is rather beyond me. He went on to give it as his opinion that it was an ideal presentment of a poet; but, as Desmond MacCarthy well observed, the sunken upper lip shows that the poet has lost his teeth. And I think we may assume that a full complement of teeth may reasonably be expected in an idealised representation of a poet.

PEARSON: Incidentally, this is clearly the man of the Droeshout portrait. The nose, the mouth, the forehead, of course, and even the eyes are all Droeshout's, but instead of a lifeless effigy this is a living man. It's wonderful, and the whole world will have to accept it one day as the breathing image of the greatest of all men.

KINGSMILL: They're taking their time over it, just as you took yours. I've often wondered about the experiences of the Italian priest before he was interned in the Isle of Man. I presume he'd been sent over in the expectation that he would return with a very large sum for the monastery, and I can only hope that his superiors in Rome accepted with Christian trust his assurance that while it would have been a simple enough matter to dispose of the canvas and frame by themselves, the fact that the canvas was disfigured by England's greatest glory was making it difficult to find a purchaser. You may remember, Clifford, telling me that although your writing friends all accepted it as genuine, the only ripple from the outside world has been an offer from a gentleman in Southwark, who wished to sell you a portrait of Lord Nelson. But Pearson and I will do our best. May we call it the Clifford Bax Shakespeare in our book? I don't believe in chance; you are the agent through whom it has become known to us, and it is our duty to tell the world, just as it is the world's duty to buy our books.

CLIFFORD BAX: I am afraid that duty has not quite the attraction for me that I am glad to see it has for you, but, as you say, there is perhaps more than chance in the train of events which has put me, who have written a play on Lord Nithsdale, in possession of his portrait of Shakespeare.

Thanking their host very warmly for his hospitality, and raising no objection to John Trevor pouring them out a final libation, they took their leave.

On the afternoon of July 4, Pearson and Kingsmill took the three forty-four for Lowestoft from Liverpool Street Station. They had a compartment to themselves, and Kingsmill remarked "I ran into an old friend this morning with whom I was at Oxford. He is the head of a family business in the city. His real interest is in literature, but he inherited the business from his father, and has carried it on very ably and conscientiously for the past twenty years. When I asked him how he was faring under the present Government, he said that it was trying to be treated all the time like a criminal, and that was the attitude of the Government to the class which was once considered the mainstay of the country and the source of its prosperity. I sympathised with him, and said that there was always some class which was made responsible for all the sufferings of mankind. Yesterday priests and kings were the scapegoats, now it was the capitalists, and one could only hope that the next on the roster would be the bureaucrat.

PEARSON: In the Victorian age the villain of the piece was the fornicator. Now he's the financier.

KINGSMILL: And just as a theoretical disapproval of fornication had no effect on its practice, so the present cant about money-making prevents no one from getting as much cash as he can. The new Puritans who see financial immorality everywhere are as obsessed with money as the old Puritans who saw sexual immorality everywhere were obsessed with sex. Personally I prefer the old Puritans to the new, for if one must be forever brooding on one thing, let it be girls not graft.

PEARSON: Talking of finance, have you ever made your will?

KINGSMILL: Yes, but don't let me stop you talking of finance. I take it you've just made your will.

PEARSON: No, but a visit to Battle yesterday reminded me of when I did. Never having had any cash, it didn't occur to me to make a will till 1944 when I was living in the middle of the coastal area over which the flying bombs were being shot out of the sky like rocketing pheasants—one of the measures for safeguarding London on which the Prime Minister dwelt with a satisfaction which we didn't altogether share. So I called on Fred Sheppard, who being both the chief solicitor and coroner of the district, was clearly my man. He glanced at the rough draft I had made and said "There's nothing here about cremation. Do you wish to be cremated?" "Not a bad idea," I said. "But as I am making a will just now because I might at any moment be exploded by a flying bomb, perhaps a cremation clause is unnecessary." "Certainly not," said Sheppard. "You may wish to have the bits assembled and then incinerated." "I hadn't thought of that," I said. "Then," said Sheppard, "shall we say—to be cremated if collected?" I should add that my friend Sheppard conducted this enquiry as he would have conducted the gathering of my fragments, with urbane solicitude.

The train passed along the southern ridge of the Constable valley and skirted the Broads, where Kingsmill excitedly drew his friend's attention to white sails floating over the distant fields—an effect, Pearson said, by which he had been much struck on his first visit to those parts over forty years ago.

They soon felt at home in their Lowestoft hotel, the Hatfield, and after dinner, which ended to their great comfort with strawberries and cream, strolled contentedly southwards to the end of the esplanade.

PEARSON: It's pleasant, but a little mournful, that low, dark line of cliffs. One misses the white steep cliffs of the South Coast, which even on a dull day give a brightness to the scene.

KINGSMILL: Those cliffs seem to be failing with age, dwindling back from the sea, as though their exhausted nerves found the sea too boisterous a neighbour.

PEARSON: Even those houses up there are crumbling away. That isn't bomb damage. It's sea encroachment, which is eating away the very foundations.

KINGSMILL: But what about that church farther in? Sea encroachment doesn't unroof a church, or does it?

PEARSON: That is decrepitude. There isn't a church in Suffolk which isn't as old as the Fens.

A passer-by, on being asked by Kingsmill whether any bombs had ever been dropped thereabouts, replied that all the damage within view had been done by bombs. "I thought so," said Pearson. "Thank you."

BLUNDESTON

Before leaving London Pearson had consulted Forster's *Life of Dickens*, and discovered that Blundeston, described by J. W. T. Ley, Forster's editor, as "a charming village a few miles from Yarmouth", was the original of Blunderstone, the scene of David Copperfield's childhood. Kingsmill welcoming his suggestion that they should take Blundeston on the way to Yarmouth, the travellers set forth by car at eleven o'clock on the morning after their arrival.

PEARSON: I've always wanted to see this country, because the early part of *David Copperfield* is the best description of childhood in English fiction. There is a wonderful charm about it.

KINGSMILL: The details are really delightful. He was happy only as a child, and the rectory at Blunderstone, though it doubtless owes a good deal to Dickens's visit to Blundeston, has always seemed to me an idealised picture of his own home at Chatham. But Yarmouth, which he saw for the first time on this visit, is very vividly done too. Arnold and I were there on holiday fifty years ago, and I have a kind of recollection of a dark street some way back from the front, and a low shore and the smell of fish, and mixed with all this the later impression of David's meal in the inn on his way to London, and the waiter who polished it off for him. It says a lot for Dickens's power over the English imagination that, although I believe he was in Yarmouth only for a day or two, everyone, except perhaps the natives of the place, thinks of Dickens when Yarmouth is mentioned.

PEARSON: It certainly must have been his early memories that make the first part of *David Copperfield* so charming, for the magnet that drew him to these parts, I learned from Forster, was a peculiarly atrocious crime which had just occurred near Norwich, the murder of Jeremy, Recorder of that city, by one Rush. It was Dickens who fixed on Norwich for a jaunt with some friends, and he did so in order to gloat over the scene of the murder and also the place of execution. From Norwich he went on to Yarmouth which, says Forster, he 'made the home of little Emily.'

Their driver, a red-faced weather-beaten little man, as taciturn as Barkis and, it may be, had he been given sufficient time, as willing, drew up outside Blundeston church. To the astonishment of the travellers, there was no sign of a house of any kind nearby, and the church itself, instead of being homely, tranquil and ivy-covered, with rooks cawing in the elms and jackdaws croaking from the eaves, was a bleak Saxon edifice, with a gaunt round tower which evoked a dim, wolf-haunted England, wattled huts and natives clad in sheepskins. Going round the church, the travellers saw to the north a field of corn, on the farther side of which they could discern a few scattered houses and a mill—but still no rectory. In the churchyard nettles were growing, and long grasses half covered the tombstones, which were leaning in all directions. The interior of the church was well kept, but in spite of its neatness and orderliness there was an air of melancholy in the place. "If the windows were all of stained glass," said Pearson, "the general effect wouldn't be depressing. But the light is too bright for this bare interior."

Returning to the car they were driven to the rectory, and walked up the drive towards a commodious early

nineteenth-century building, a stream below them to the
right and on their left a plot of grass with trees and thickets
round it.

"No wonder," said Kingsmill, who had *David Copperfield*
with him, "that Dickens writes–'There comes out of the
cloud, our house . . .' This place, if he ever saw it,
which I doubt, contributed nothing to his description of
David's home and his surroundings. He speaks of David
looking out of his bedroom window on to the quiet churchyard, with the dead all lying in their graves at rest, below
the solemn moon. 'There is,' he says, 'nothing half so
green that I know anywhere, as the grass of that churchyard; nothing half so shady
as its trees; nothing half so
quiet as its tombstones.'
But grass, however green,
trees, however shady, and
tombstones, be they never so
quiet, do not individualise a
place.

PEARSON: And, in any
case, even if the hedge we
saw round the churchyard
wasn't there in Dickens's
time, and these trees here

93, *Cheyne Walk*, (*Mrs. Gaskell*)

had not been planted, David could only have descried
the tombstones with the aid of Peggotty's telescope.
One doesn't expect topographical exactitude from a
novelist; but if he borrows the name of a definite place,
he ought to aim at *some* kind of resemblance."

KINGSMILL: Mrs. Gaskell didn't claim that a visit to
Stonehenge had inspired her to write *Cranford*, and I

think Dickens might have exercised a similar restraint. It's a little hard that when you and I cross half England to sweeten our thoughts of Dickens with a sight of one of the few oases in his Sahara of gloom and horror, he should doublecross us like this.

PEARSON: Why did Ley talk about the charming village of Blundeston, as if everything were according to Dickens's specifications—the village clustering round the rectory and the rectory clustering round the church? Was he acting under instructions from the Dickens Fellowship? Is there a Secret Three or Seven that decides what's to be done in these cases? Is bluff used on one occasion, and candour where bluff won't serve?

48, Doughty Street, Dickens Fellowship Headquarters

KINGSMILL: I'm a little sorry for the Dickens Fellowship these days. They've had to take some hard knocks these last ten years. A mistress and a child of shame. . . .

PEARSON: A wife's broken heart and a daughter's curses. . .

KINGSMILL: What next? Well, if they turn to me for comfort, I shall cheer them with Abraham Lincoln's famous slogan, transposing it slightly so as to bring out more clearly than Abe saw fit to do its message of reassurance to the directing minds of all societies and fellowships, churches and political parties. . . Though you cannot fool all the people all the time, you can fool all the people some of the time, and some of the people all the time.

They drove into Yarmouth; Barkis put them down at the Queen's Hotel, overcharged them and went off. While waiting for lunch they sat on the front.

PEARSON: This is the most degraded seaside place I have ever seen in my life. Blackpool, an inferno of vulgarity, has yet a kind of monstrous magnificence. Bexhill, just because it is completely nondescript, is not painful enough to call for description. But this!–Look left, and you see a lot of red-brick late Victorian buildings which in any other place would make you glad to turn sharply to the right. But here, if you are so ill-advised as to turn to the right, what do you see? That ghastly pavilion with its pillars crowned by those nightmare helmets. I call them helmets because they look like the kind of head-gear which a Gestapo agent serving the Mikado might wear if he were a hundred foot high and had been begotten by Edgar Allan Poe. As for this front, it's just a clutter of nothingness which yet contrives to daze one with its superlative ugliness. That is all–for the time being.

KINGSMILL: Steerforth's luck held to the end. He was dead when he washed up here. I have had a faint nostalgia for Yarmouth for fifty years. It is cured. Even the sea looks confined and gloomy, those ships labouring heavily as in a dream, bound for nowhere . . .

PEARSON: Drifting aimlessly in No Man's Water.

Refreshed by lunch, they emerged from the hotel in a more cheerful humour, Pearson modifying "degraded" into "disreputable" as he took another look round. The sight of horse-drawn landaus carried them back half a century–some of them standing in a rank, others ambling along the front with beaming cargoes of elderly women. "As I have had occasion to remark before," said Pearson, "we are all children of God; but we've got to get out of here pretty quickly all the same." They hailed a taxi and once within it felt sufficiently secure to face a ride round the town.

As they drove southwards, their driver, a willing and communicative youth, pointed to a statue on a high column. It was Britannia, he said; and its sculptor, when he realised that she was facing inland instead of towards the sea, had committed suicide. Kingsmill queried the driver's explanation, pointing out that the responsibility for locating the direction in which the sea lay must have been divided between some scores of persons, but that the responsibility for Britannia herself rested entirely on the sculptor, and was, so far as he could judge in passing, a very valid reason for suicide. As the houses of Gorleston became visible beyond the Yare, Pearson exclaimed "Now that really is delightful! Any painter would love those old roofs rising one above the other from the river's edge." They circled back into Yarmouth, drove over the cobbles of the South Quay past houses between two and three hundred years old, and were shocked at the sudden sight of bomb devastation, which seemed to them at least as bad as any-thing in London. Driving through the Market Square, where Kingsmill was vaguely conscious of early impressions which Pearson did not trouble him to clarify, they came to the famous Parish Church. It had been completely gutted by incendiary bombs. They got out and walked round it through an old churchyard with high banks and over-shadowing trees, a beautiful though melancholy place. "This," said Pearson, "was the largest parish church in

England, with one exception, St. Michael's, Coventry,
which later became a cathedral, and is now also destroyed."

Nearby the church was a house with an inscription which
they read with pensive interest—

> Mrs. Sewell authoress of Mother's Last Words
> Resided here.
> Her daughter Anna of Black Beauty Fame
> Was born here 30 March 1820.

When they reached Lowestoft their driver overcharged
them much more outrageously than had Barkis. Concealing
his surprise, Pearson paid up like a gentleman, and rejoined
Kingsmill, who was regretting that he had not intervened
like a man.

KINGSMILL: We've paid for our vanity, and naturally will
not get what we've paid for.

PEARSON: It's going to be his day's comic story. What we
would like him to say in the pub to-night is—"You don't
often meet a couple like that. Perfect gents, free-handed,
friendly, interested in everything." What he will say is—
"A pair of suckers! You don't often meet a couple like
that."

LOVABLE WRITERS

Sitting in the sunshine the next morning, in the garden in
front of the Hatfield, the friends, Dickens still lingering
in their minds, discussed who among famous writers was
and who was not lovable.

PEARSON: Most of them are about fifty-fifty. Smollett,

for example, was obviously a cantankerous fellow, but sincere and courageous; and Galsworthy had plenty of public spirit but not much private geniality.

KINGSMILL: And Gibbon doesn't warm to himself, so no one else can. And Southey claims so much from one's esteem that one is too exhausted to offer any affection.

PEARSON: It's far easier to be definite about who is lovable than about who is unlovable. One may dislike a man for certain reasons, but he's bound to have some merits and that takes the edge off one's antipathy. But if a man's lovable, even his faults are attractive, and one can go full steam ahead. Now, to take one of the unlovables, Sterne has never appealed to me. He was a snivelling, affected, callous humbug, the inventor of the tear-behind-the-smile technique, which has dried the tears and withered the smiles of every decent man in the last two hundred years. Does this mean that I am blind to his good points? I wonder.

KINGSMILL: There are some very fine lines in *Modern Love*, but on the whole I dislike Meredith even more than Sterne. He was conceited, snobbish, contorted and cruel, and loved Mother Nature so passionately that he could only express himself in a style which makes Congreve read like a Border Ballad. Compared with Meredith, Dickens moves one's sympathy if not one's affection. At least he didn't pretend his inferno was an Eden.

PEARSON: We're not making much headway with the good points of the unlovable, so I will reserve my opinion of Milton, Pope, Tennyson, Browning and Kipling for the present, and pass to the lovable ones. While freely admitting that Shakespeare was a sycophant in the company of peers—

KINGSMILL: And Johnson altogether too obliging at the table of Mr. Thrale—

PEARSON: And Scott revoltingly servile with George IV—

KINGSMILL: And the manly Fielding supple enough while easing Allen of cash—

PEARSON: And Sydney Smith in Mayfair a disgrace to his cloth—

KINGSMILL: And Thackeray a boneless blunder from most angles—

PEARSON: Are these the lads we love?

KINGSMILL: Well, there's beggary in the love that can be reckoned.

PEARSON: A fat lot of consolation they'd get out of that if they were listening-in.

VALEDICTORY

It was Thursday, July 11, and the travellers, who were having tea in the Club, decided that Thursday, July 11, was a good day on which to round off their travels. "Let's go up to Hampstead Heath," said Pearson, "and take farewell of London from the spot of all others where one can best survey the greatest city in the world."

They went by tube, and turning down Flask Walk reached the Heath. Strolling along by the pond on which Shelley used to sail paper boats for Leigh Hunt's children, and where now a few aged fishermen were brooding over their floats, they came to the Vale of Health. Outside

Leigh Hunt's house some children were playing cricket, one of whom, a pretty dark-eyed, dark-haired child, noticed that the travellers were looking at the wall surrounding the house, and asked them if they would like to go inside. Her father and mother lived there, she said, and her name was Bagrit.

The house, which now for the first time they saw at close quarters, was a delightful little Regency building with grass-plots on two sides. "Do you realise," said Pearson, turning to the child, "that this house has had more great men of genius in it than any other house in the world—Wordsworth, Coleridge, Keats, Shelley, Hazlitt and Lamb?"

"Oh, yes," the child answered. "Everyone knows that. *Millions* of people are *always* looking down on our house from that hill there."

As they went up towards Jack Straw's Castle, Pearson illustrated for his friend the various styles of walking favoured by Leigh Hunt's visitors: Wordsworth shambling majestically, his feet for the most part turned outwards, but occasionally turned inwards, perhaps in obedience to some metaphysical principle of his own; Coleridge, hands folded on his ample belly, his eyes cast upwards, his feet prudently exploring the surest way over the uneven ground; Hazlitt straggling mistrustfully; Shelley, head forward, breaking every now and then into little runs; Lamb precise and delicate, with spasms of uncertainty; Keats, five foot high, striding along, erect and martial.

They reached a grove of scattered pines, from which in clear weather they had often seen the dome of St. Paul's high above the white towers and spires of the city; but now a haze veiled everything beyond the Heath.

PEARSON: So much for our valediction to the great town to which we have dedicated a year of loving service and unsparing toil.

KINGSMILL: This neighbourhood seems unpropitious to set occasions. I remember going up to Highgate on September 8, 1944. The flying bombs had just ceased, Germany, I thought, was practically finished, and I wanted to look over London and muse on its great deliverance. My reverie was shattered by a gigantic explosion. It was the first of the rocket bombs.

Leaving the grove, the friends walked down to Church Row, discussing on the way whether it was more agreeable to be delivered from peace by war or from war by peace.